The Lord of the
SILENCE

ISBN: 978-1-5272-9302-1

Published by: Peoples Publishing Limited

71-75 Shelton Street, London, Greater London WC2H 9JQ

A private limited company in England and Wales, Company Registration Number 12839076.

Shaneenclarke.com and The Lord of the Silence book copyright is owned and managed by Peoples Publishing Limited, a Private Limited Company in England & Wales, Company Registration Number 12839076.

Printed in the United States of America.

The Lord of the SILENCE

Experiencing intimacy with God in this fast-paced world

SHANEEN CLARKE

Dedication

This book is dedicated to all those seeking solitude and silence in the midst of noise and chaos.

For those readers looking for the oasis in the desert of modern-day life, I place this book in your hands to take away the hurry and harangue of this 21st-century world.

Come and experience with me the Silence that only The Lord of the Silence can bring and let Him become your ever constant source of joy and peace in the days to come.

Shaneen Clarke

Introduction

Many years ago, a friend of mine invited me to attend a meeting. I accepted the invitation and, when we arrived, we made our way into a packed room with noise levels that can only be described as irritating. The constant onslaught of the clamour and roar throughout the meeting was exhausting. As soon as the meeting came to an end, I excused my self and left by way of the nearest exit. I wandered through the hustle and bustle of London's streets, with the constant din of the traffic and the background noises barking at me as I made my way back home.

Moments later, I opened my front door and stepped through the doorway. As I closed the door behind me, I breathed a sigh of relief as I stood there, motionless, taking in the silence. Savouring the quiet atmosphere, which was so welcoming and stood in stark contrast to the buzz of the gathering I had just attended, I felt as if I had come out of a turbulent tunnel of noise and emerged into a peaceful open plain. Immersed in the stillness with only the sound of my own breath piercing the quiet, I realised The Lord of the Silence was beckoning me.

That experience inspired a quest for a greater understanding of silence. My journey began as I researched the topic and read about monks who lived a life of silence, committing every waking moment to seeking to listen and wait.

The monk's disciplined life of silence encompasses quietness where there is no absence of words or thoughts. They practise their silent reflection throughout the day along with their vow of poverty. In some circles, the practice has been applied differently, and they have mingled their own gods with Buddhism and Hinduism.

The Lord of the Silence is mentioned in Psalm 109:1, which says, "O God of my praise, Do not be silent!" True silence is not just the absence of noise. Silence embraced for spiritual reasons opens up the hidden presence of God in our lives, and it is an inexplicable presence and one to pursue. The Lord of the Silence must be encountered on a spiritual level... never explained akin to a love within a good marriage as they experience the blessing of their union.

I stumbled onto the 46th Psalm of David, verse 10, which says, "Be still and know that I am God," which I meditated upon and pondered for weeks. As I meditated on that verse, I realised that silence is an invitation, not an obligation. In my prayer time, I began to remain in silence and sow the seeds of contemplation into the weave of my life. My hunger for stillness increased and my pursuit of silence became my haven as I entered new depths with greater, more in-depth revelations.

My new life began to unfold. I began to encourage my peers and friends to pursue silence. I started groups called 'Listening Ear', and we would practise being still and listen together. This began to change lives in a way that my friends, peers and I had not seen before, introducing us to the importance and benefits of silence. As the change happening within grew in intensity, I realised that The Lord of the Silence was unlocking the door to a new dimension of communion in sacred silence. And I began to understand that anyone going forward in a world of faster pace and louder volumes who would undertake the journey would be equipped with a greater perspective and wider vision to truly comprehend the meaning of "Be still and know".

Contents

"

There is no better time to begin the journey with
The Lord of the Silence than right now!

Chapter 1

The Call of Silence

London is an amazing city, and I realise now that growing up there was a wonderful experience. When I think about my childhood, my mind is flooded with fond memories of the sights, sounds and smells that were such a part of my life and made up the backdrop of our neighbourhood.

We lived near the Mother's Pride bread factory and the lovely aroma of fresh bread baking often hung in the air. I can still remember the mouth-watering smell of the bread that blanketed our neighbourhood whenever the factory was in production. With fresh bread so close at hand, I would bring freshly baked loaves of bread to our neighbours from time to time, and they always received it with a welcoming smile.

The halls of my childhood memories still echo with the familiar sounds of my early surroundings. When I reflect on them, I can still hear them today... like the noisy London buses. For as long as I can remember, much of London's population has relied on the London buses, which were far noisier years ago than they are currently. Added to noisy buses stopping and starting on our street was 'hop-on, hop-off' platform, manned by a bus conductor who consistently barked out orders at people as loudly as possible while they tried to get on the bus.

Not far from our home there were a number of market stalls, which were more prominent in appearance and presence at that time than today's shops are. The market stalls were always manned by traders with loud, captivating voices, especially during the weekends when the number of shoppers was at its peak. The booming voices of the traders, combined with the patrons milling about the market stalls and making their purchases, added to the noise and activity in the area. Generally speaking, there was always a constant din of noise in the streets that was loud and lewd.

I was born into a large, loving family. In addition to my mother and father, I had three siblings – an older brother, a sister and a younger brother. I also grew up alongside two nephews and two nieces and my sister-in-law's grandmother lived with us too. At one point, my uncle and aunt also moved in with us, so my father bought the adjoining house to accommodate our ever-expanding family.

My father was a chiropractor, and our house was always flooded with emergency patients coming and going. The doorbell rang incessantly and if my father was not at home, his desperate patients waited for him to return. To maintain our code of family hospitality, tea was always served to them to make their wait more comfortable.

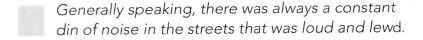

Generally speaking, there was always a constant din of noise in the streets that was loud and lewd.

In addition to the comings and goings of family and extended family living in our home, we also had a dog and a cat. I remember the time the cat gave birth to seven kittens, which we eventually gave away as gifts to neighbours in our immediate community.

Our Neighbourhood

We lived in a somewhat noisy neighbourhood, so whether I was at home or walking about in the neighbourhood, there always seemed to be a buzz of activity and sounds nearby. I didn't realise it in my early years, but even then, I believe I was searching for The Lord of the Silence on some level; looking for solitude in some of my favourite places like the nearby grounds of the local vicarage, my tree house, or my neighbour's garden. The English maintained beautiful front and rear gardens to their homes and it was lovely to enjoy the changing seasons amidst their incredibly groomed lawns and blooming flowers. In these times, there was a sense of real community and safety; consequently, stealing away for a few quiet moments of solace to enjoy the neighbour's garden or one of my other special places of solitude brought a welcome reprieve from the myriad of background noises in the neighbourhood and in our home on any given day, allowing me to still my soul as I basked in the silence.

It was also quite common for people in our community to own dogs. Free to roam at will and ready to bark at anything that moved, it was standard fare to hear dogs barking early in the morning, signalling the arrival of a whistling milkman making his morning deliveries. The same response happened when our bread and the post were delivered. Although this was how bread, milk and the post arrived every day, that delivery system joined in unison to create a mayhem of morning madness. I can also remember the ration man in post-war Britain who would deliver the box of groceries regularly, which was a weekly highlight. My siblings and I befriended this wonderful man because he brought us such joy with fizzy drinks included.

Another regular occurrence was the arrival of the mobile library, which came to our street every week. The familiar sound of its arrival was a pleasant sound to my ears because I loved pouring through the books in the large steel vehicle. I remember discovering books like Robin Hood, Janet and John and Alice in Wonderland, which is one of my favourites. It was written by Lewis Carroll, and years later I learned that he actually preached in a church opposite our place in the country. Though noisy, our neighbourhood provided a beautiful setting for my upbringing in so many ways with such rich culture and generous spirit by all who lived nearby.

Burly builders from beyond our neighbourhood seemed to be consistently present as they carved out a new London, adding another layer of noise to the already buzzing background of sounds. Joined with all these sounds was another familiar sound – the systematic ringing of Big Ben's chimes emerging from the shadows of the city that framed its silhouette in the distance, the distinctly recognisable bells wafting their way across London's picturesque canvas like a gentle breeze.

A New Awareness

As a child and even later as an adult, I didn't give much thought to London's historic Big Ben or the distinct sound of its bells; it was just part of London's background noise. But as the busyness of life swelled up around me like waves on the ocean, I began to sense the tug of The Lord of the Silence. I undertook a study of the topic of stillness from Scripture, and as I pursued my studies, I came to realise that the bells I had heard every day of my life represented so much more to me than just the scheduled ringing of a bell. I discovered that the daily toll of these familiar bells had sounded a call to silence decades earlier; an historic call of The Lord of the Silence that changed the world.

London's Silent Minute

The Silent Minute was an historic movement that began in 1940 inspired by Major Wellesley Tudor Pole OBE during the Second World War blitz on the UK. Historical accounts say that the major perceived the inner request from a high spiritual source that there be a Silent Minute of Prayer for Freedom, observed at 9 pm each evening during the striking of Big Ben. He believed if enough people joined in this gesture of dedicated intent, the tide would turn and the invasion of England would be diverted.

Major Tudor Pole's inspiration for this dedicated minute of silence received the direct support of King George VI, Sir Winston Churchill, and his parliamentary cabinet. It was also recognised by US President Franklin D. Roosevelt and observed on land and at sea on the battlefields, in air raid shelters and in hospitals. With Churchill's support, the BBC began to play the bells of Big Ben on the radio on Sunday, November 10, 1940, as a signal for the Silent Minute to begin. From that day on, people would unite each day at 9 pm for one minute in meditation, prayer or focus and consciously will for peace to prevail.

Major Tudor Pole said, "There is no power on earth that can withstand the united cooperation on spiritual levels of men and women of goodwill everywhere. It is for this reason that the continued and widespread observance of the Silent Minute is of such vital importance in the interest of human welfare."

The Prevailing Power of The Lord of the Silence

The Silent Minute was unconventional, yet effective, especially when implemented on a national level with its impact reaching beyond the shores of Britain. The profound power of this silence was recognised and reported by a British intelligence officer in 1945 while interrogating a high Nazi official. During the interrogation, the officer asked, "Why do you think Germany lost the war?" The Nazi official responded by saying, "During the war, you had a secret weapon for which we could find no countermeasure, which we did not understand, but it was very powerful. It was associated with the striking of Big Ben each evening. I believe you called it 'The Silent Minute'."

Some people have attributed the power of the Silent Minute to group meditation. Others acknowledge it as corporate agreement in prayer for a desired result. Whatever your viewpoint may be, there is an indescribable, immeasurable power present when The Lord of the Silence comes on the scene.

Some people have continued the habit of the 9 pm. prayer ever since the Second World War, but have diverted their focus to the different areas of the world wherever there are ongoing conflicts. Apart from these few people, the practice had been largely forgotten by the British public for almost half a century until it was revived.

The Silent Minute Today

The Silent Minute was revived by Dorothy Forster and gained a new following of people after the 9/11 terrorist attack on the World Trade Center in New York City on September 11, 2001. The commencement of the wars in Iraq and Afghanistan also brought new Silent Minute participants forward. It continues as a small charitable organisation based in London, but with a worldwide list of participants.

The Call of Silence

My search for The Lord of the Silence began a few years ago and was born out of the storm of noise in which I found myself entrenched. My journey happens to have begun in London but wasn't based on the city itself; it had much more to do with the hushed whisper of The Lord of the Silence calling me to a place of stillness.

The call to silence can happen anywhere, at any time, and through any avenue. The Silent Minute called to a nation and beyond, and The Lord of the Silence stepped into history and changed the world. My quest started out of the noisy mayhem in my life.

Your journey in life up to this point may or may not have similarities to mine. And the battle that you're facing may have nothing to do with the place you live, Big Ben, Winston Churchill, or mirror any of the details of my story. Your struggles could be based on any variety of challenges and the noise that holds you captive could resonate from any number of things in your life. It doesn't matter if your battle is against the clock of insufficient time, or a conflict in your life over your marriage, finances or debt, or just being you. Whatever struggle you're facing today – whatever 'noise' is holding you captive – I have good news: there is hope for you. I encourage you to take a moment to find a quiet place, a sanctuary of silence like I found as a child in my neighbour's garden or on the grounds of the local vicarage, a place of refuge where you can be still and commune with The Lord of the Silence.

Beginning the Journey

Before you read another page of this book or allow one more minute to be stolen from you by the noise in your life, pause, take a deep breath, and together, let's commit your battle to God. This is the first step in answering the call of silence. The Bible says, "The Lord will fight your battle for you" (Exodus 14:14). God's promises are more certain than tomorrow's sunrise, and He promises to fight your battle for you, regardless of what the battle may be. Remember, no battle is too big or too small for God. All you have to do is give it to Him.

Are you ready to hand your battle over to the Lord and begin to rest in quiet stillness, knowing He will fight for you? Don't delay because there's no better time to begin the journey with The Lord of the Silence than right now!

The Lord of the Silence is always waiting to meet us and carry us through if we will learn to be still.

Chapter 2

In Search of Silence

Is it possible to find silence in the midst of today's noisy world? This is a question to which I had never given much conscious consideration until I began my quest for The Lord of the Silence. Living in London, the capital city of England and also the most populated city in Great Britain, with more than 13,600 people per square mile, it's understandable that silence is a rare commodity.

On the other hand, noise is part of life. We are born with two ears as everything comes in stereo. Many things, including stress, one of the biggest silent killers of the 21st century, is intensified by the noise levels around us. This includes the constant switching on and plugging into electrical devices in the surround sound of the inner cities and the clatter, chatter and banter of our environment. Whichever way we turn, we come face to face with noise, and the levels of its intrusive presence in the world are increasing.

Where Do We Begin?

The pinging and ringing of mobile devices, along with the alerts and alarms of these seemingly necessary but invasive devices on which we have become so dependent, create a cacophony of sound. The iPod , iPad and iPhone clamour for attention in this populous world of over 7 billion, with over 20% glued to Facebook, the 23 million emails per minute that are sent, and the 92 million monthly YouTube visits – all competing for our attention. On buses, on trains, in coffee shops, there is no escape. We are all herded around in an abstract bubble of noise with no way out.

People are seeking different ways to relax and reduce stress, to chill and be still. The motto of Sussex University is 'Be still and Know', adopted by Lord Fulton from Psalm 46 in the year 1961 when incidentally student fees were £55 per annum and the world a much quieter place.

The media culture is seeking to tailor-make our lives around social media with its various and stylish gadgets of access. People want to keep each other at a distance so that they can be in control. We are becoming increasingly used to being alone in a together but not together world. More and more, there is a preference to text not talk, tweet not meet, and we expect more from technology than the very people we link with.

We are lonely but afraid of intimacy with people, though in the moment of being still, there rises within us a sense of panic. This modern dichotomy is being calmed by the presence of those gadgets used to connect and the knowledge that everyone we know is a digital transmission away. By talking too much with our friends we may spoil the fun and best limit our connect to short speak of no more than 140 characters.

Busy, Bustling London

Because London is my home, I use it as an example. Multiply all the pinging, dinging and alerts you experience every day by 12 million plus, which is the current population of the greater London area… and try to imagine the challenge of finding silence. It's like trying to find a needle in a haystack!

In addition to being one of the world's leading financial centres for international business and commerce, London enjoys the status of having one of the largest city economies in the world. Within the square mile of the city, over 400,000 people are coming and going to work on a daily basis. London is also a major tourism attraction internationally. With its thousand-year history and over 35 million visitors to the city last year, tourism adds to the never-ending buzzing activity in the city.

The Common Thread

London's residents come from every part of the globe, yet one common thread ties them together: the noise level that visually and mentally inundates their lives. In fact, the noise is regarded as pollution, and the Corporation of London is looking for ways to reduce the decibels. Road noise is just one of the sources, and more than 1.6 million people in the city are exposed to levels above 55db during the day, the level defined by the World Health Organisation as causing health problems. The non-stop road traffic noise of London is compounded by the congestion of homes, restaurants, building sites, commercial plants and machinery, chatter, and overhead aircraft in the city... all coming together as an overpowering discordant sound to cope with on the crowded streets.

The Quest for Silence

With its constant hustle and bustle of activity, London is the antithesis of silence. A cacophony of sounds from different languages, bumper to bumper traffic, building sites, road works and the constant din of emergency services and mobile phones in motion combine to become an endless epiphany of rushing activity. The relentless noise is killing us and to survive its onslaught, we must pursue silence at all costs.

Silent rooms are being created in public places and on trains where noise is forbidden and the solitude of sound is bound. In the midst of London's swirling, endless noise, silence is an elusive commodity, and when found, is like an oasis in the desert.

Living in constant noise or being immersed in it for the better part of each day can become so common and familiar that it feels 'normal' in some distorted way and is somehow reassuring. But silence can bring peace or it can become a force that distorts reality. I met a still model by chance in an Oxford coffee shop while writing this book who told me that when she models for a sculpture, she is exposed to a silence which she finds threatening and, at times, panic can set in. She begins to think negative thoughts and becomes perplexed with the silence of the sculptor, wondering if anything is wrong in the moment or if she had done something to upset the artist as he perfects his work.

The silence to seek, however, is one that brings peace. But from where does the silence that brings peace come? It is not a mantra or elevated plain but a hunger for which the human soul longs that is released from heaven. In the pursuit of silence and through His presence, it is a ringtone that comes from within and a divine wireless connection.

What does this peace bring? The model I speak of tapped into a reservoir of negativity and chaos against the silence of passion and purpose. To quiet your thoughts, silence gives strength and fruitfulness as it invigorates us and develops us. In silence, as we reflect upon Scripture, we develop not only our spiritual life but also bring renewal within as the word within us is stored to flow out of us. Unless we are filled, how can we possibly flow? Silence is like a battery charger for you and me, just like the mode of your phone as it is charged in the silence of the night, ready to pour forth the next morning.

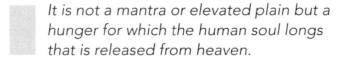

It is not a mantra or elevated plain but a hunger for which the human soul longs that is released from heaven.

We need to gain back the ground that has been lost, to cultivate solitude and to find our real self. We need to reclaim our space with God, and in the stillness of this connect, stop and behold His wonder. In time, we will create the open space that will lead to us being reinvigorated in the pasture and streams of a refreshed emotional and spiritual life.

The Strength of Silence

A few years ago I was called upon to introduce Cherie Blair, wife of former prime minister Tony Blair, at The Woman's Call, an organisation whose vision is to empower women in business, the corporate place and in influence, in order to reach people and see the transformation of life. The setting for the event was the Ritz London, which is the backcloth to a divine leading which came to me in 2002. I had wondered why The Lord of the Silence was often hosted in poor-looking venues and more particularly why we were not reaching out to the London elite. With this in mind, I chose the Ritz Hotel as the setting.

The Ritz Hotel London was built by César Ritz following the completion of the Ritz Hotels in Paris and Madrid in the late 19th century. The architects Mewes and Hawkes created a superb and iconic design from a steel frame cast in Germany and splendid arcaded facades with interiors in the style of Louis XIV. The hotel is located in a prime spot at 150 Piccadilly at the corner of Arlington Street, just a short walk from Buckingham Palace, and has 136 rooms of which 25 are suites. At the rear is William Kent House which boasts six major function/dining facilities fit literally for the Queen and is the only place in London outside her palace where Her Majesty dines. It is a 5-star hotel within a Grade 2 listed building. The location of Piccadilly is, in fact, the birthplace of the Queen and is world famous, linking Hyde Park Corner to the west, to the statue of Eros on Piccadilly Circus to the east and in major part overlooking Green Park towards Buckingham Palace a stone's throw away.

The Right Setting

In the centre of the hotel is the famous Palm Court which daily serves the world-famous Ritz Tea. A Ritz Tea is the finest tea, sandwiches without crust, scones, jam and cream with patisseries extraordinaire. It is indeed a feast to behold. My plan was to use the hotel to set a Ritz Tea in the very Ritz and invite a keynote speaker to speak to circa 40 people about their faith walk and release to us what was in their heart.

In 2003 we launched our first tea, which we titled 'A Woman's Call', choosing the Marie Antoinette Suite, which could accommodate 40 people seated at four tables of ten. This mirrored room dripping with crystal chandeliers looked more befittingly Versailles than London.

Creating The Atmosphere

Over the past 16 years we have hosted a number of speakers there, from politicians, leader's wives, clerics to the Queen, and others from a variety of backgrounds. In each instance, we follow a similar format to create a welcoming atmosphere. With soft music playing, featuring an ensemble with piano, harp and stringed instruments, the invited guests enjoy high tea and conversation as they feast on the beautifully crafted delicacies served at the Ritz London.

As the tea service slowly draws to a close, the mood changes with the introduction of a special guest. Following the speech or remarks by our guest, there is a time of ministry. On one occasion, people were slain in the power of the Holy Spirit during the ministry time. The Ritz waiters and management were in shock and didn't understand what was happening. Concerned for our guests, ambulances were called because they questioned whether this demonstration was due to a potion in the tea!

With Cherie Blair seated nearby in that beautiful setting and with the tea coming to a close, knowing that it was only moments before I would stand to introduce her to speak, I found myself surrounded by a room full of women chattering and clattering, porcelain and parlance in full flow. I sat there, attempting to gather my thoughts to make the perfect introduction, but my thoughts and the magnified sounds in the room seemed to collide with the sounds of the traffic at Hyde Park Corner, an extremely busy intersection. In fact, it's said that if you can drive around Hyde Park Corner, you can drive anywhere in the world! There in the Marie Antoinette Suite, the seconds were passing and the moment for the introduction had almost arrived.

A Silent Reprieve

Unsuccessful in my endeavour to collect my thoughts, I had no other recourse but to exit to the toilet temporarily to compose myself in silence in order to pull myself together and conduct the introduction of the prime minister's wife as planned. Only with the help of The Lord of the Silence was I able to relax and find the inner stillness needed to continue. Armed with that inner strength, it was truly a memorable moment as I moved with ease toward the lectern and introduced our guest, Cherie Blair. After a round of welcoming applause by the ladies, the atmosphere in the room changed instantaneously as the guests who had been clattering and chattering with unstoppable fervour just moments earlier listened in absolute silence.

Ultimately, the name of The Lord was quite rightly lifted up in this splendid setting befitting the King of Kings. Having Cherie Blair as our guest was a delight, and the afternoon proved to be a wonderful time of sharing testimonies that are still spoken of to this day. And as the gathering drew to a close and the ladies prepared to leave that lovely setting, the hustle and bustle of activity in the London streets beyond the walls of the Ritz Hotel slowly crept back into the lives of those who had enjoyed the peaceful respite of stillness that afternoon over tea.

My recollections of that afternoon still warm my heart when I reflect on them. In retrospect, I also marvel at how a 'chance meeting' that afternoon in that intimate setting would years later become the foundation of an unexpected and unfathomable blessing for my husband and me.

Far greater than the wonderful memories of our afternoon at the

Ritz with our celebrated guest or a chance meeting that would change our lives, is the lesson I learned about The Lord of the Silence that day. Whatever life's circumstances may bring our way – be it crises with our loved ones, challenges in business, or a world pandemic – The Lord of the Silence is always waiting to meet us and carry us through if we will learn to be still and allow Him to direct our steps.

"

The beauty of silence can be compared with the rotation of a diamond: the more we rotate silence, the more we realise the many ways we can experience The Lord of the Silence.

Chapter 3

A New Kind of Silence

As one year marched into the halls of history and 2020 appeared on the scene, who could have possibly anticipated the striking contrasts that would seize the world in just a few short months? Imagine those gathered at Sydney's waterfront waiting for the iconic spectacular fireworks display at Sydney's Harbour Bridge or the millions of eager Londoners lining the Thames waterfront, waiting for Big Ben to ring out 12 resounding strokes to welcome the new year as the London Eye produced its famous swirling fireworks. What about the estimated one billion plus people from around the globe who watched as Times Square's party atmosphere came alive with a million plus people squeezed into New York City's epicentre, waiting for the 12,000 lb Waterford crystal LED ball to drop — a 100-year-old tradition?

Who could have anticipated that all this global grandeur and excitement at the stroke of midnight because a new year had begun could be so abruptly altered by a silent invader called a pandemic... a force powerful enough to reduce bustling cities to empty streets? Along with an increase in occurrences of emergency vehicles transporting the sick to hospitals and daily updates of depressing news by the media came an unexpected 'new normal' in nearly every nation on the globe!

The New Normal

When I think back on that lovely afternoon at the Ritz Tea with Cherie Blair and all the guests who were present, it seems unfathomable that events like that which were once considered 'normal' have changed so dramatically, and 'a new normal' has marched into our lives with irresistible force. Everything from work patterns, national and international commerce, basic daily hygiene routines as simple as constant handwashing, travel, schools, and our entire culture has been affected as nations all over the globe have responded to the impact of the pandemic coronavirus known as COVID-19 which broke out in 2019. The outbreak of this invisible intruder caused almost immeasurable panic globally, and without a doubt, COVID-19 has become a chapter in the history books of future generations.

Prior to the 'new normal', many people I know were so busy with life with diaries or handheld devices that scheduled meetings at ten-minute intervals and school pickups at formula one speeds. The prospect of a quiet night at home alone was not anywhere on their horizon. Then, suddenly, everything changed and life as we knew it came to a screeching halt.

What about you? Were you caught right in the middle of this chapter in history? How did this invisible foe affect you and the lives of your loved ones? Will history include you among those who purchased plenty of toilet rolls, hand sanitiser and tinned food? Is this how you want to be remembered?

Isolation

I trust that many confined to their homes during the coronavirus pandemic discovered that it's possible to turn an enforced lockdown at home into something memorable and something of value. Whether you're dealing with a pandemic like COVID-19 or some other kind of crisis that has changed your life and daily activities in a dramatic way, I believe you can demonstrate creativity and vision in your life during lockdown. Regardless of what the 'new normal' has brought your way, you can make it count in your life's chapter that you are writing as you live each day.

Lessons In Lockdown

Regardless of where you call home, it's likely that the sudden onset of lockdown connected with the COVID-19 pandemic brought a measure of panic and uncertainty. The lives of multitudes around the world were suddenly and unexpectedly accosted by an invisible foe, and hearts were seized with the kind of panic one feels when you hear the blaring sound of an ambulance racing toward a crowd of people. In my own neighbourhood, I watched faces etched with deep concern as the urgency to buy necessities drove them to pack their trollies at the local market with food, drink and most importantly, the toilet rolls. (Who would have ever dreamed that our bottoms would become so important during a worldwide crisis?)

Around this time, I bumped into my elderly neighbour and we started to talk. When I mentioned the trollies filled with toilet rolls, my neighbour said in a calm, steady voice, "Shaneen, no need to panic. I have hundreds of toilet rolls in my shed. If you need any, let me know."

Surprised to learn of her stockpile, I responded by saying, "Hundreds of rolls? How come?" "Well," she said, "I bought them last summer on sale. I never thought in a million years they would become such a special commodity." As she spoke, my neighbour's words expressed peace rather than panic... perhaps because she felt prepared with her stack of toilet rolls for what might be ahead. In contrast to my neighbour who was very calm, others with whom I spoke were panic-stricken, fearing they would never have enough toilet rolls for themselves, let alone any extra to share with anyone else. Surprisingly, some people were totally oblivious and laid back. They appeared to take everything in their stride... as if absolutely nothing had changed.

Personally, it all seemed too much: the casual apathy of some in contrast to the extreme anxiety I saw in others related to the scene at the market as people prepared for what they feared was ahead. I chose to switch off for a while, connect with myself, and embrace the pause of 'the new normal' that had come upon us without warning.

Who On Earth Created Quarantine?

The restriction on the movement of people and goods during the 'new normal' was labelled quarantine. Intended to prevent the spread of disease, people's activities quickly ground to a halt.

As I looked into it, I learned that this 'isolation' sense of quarantine comes from the Italian quarantina, a period of forty days, derived from quadrant the Italian for 'forty'. So what's so special about 40? Historically, a quarantine referred to a period of time – originally 40 days – imposed upon ships when suspected of carrying an infectious or contagious disease. This practice was done in Venice in the 1300s in an effort to stave off the plague.

Regardless of what the 'new normal' has brought your way, you can make it count in your life's chapter that you are writing as you live each day

This makes me think of Noah, who must have felt quarantined inside the ark as he sheltered in place to preserve human life, which consisted of his family. God quarantined Noah and his family, along with a boatload of animals. Essentially, Noah was in lockdown just as people all over the world were when COVID-19 came knocking.

The COVID-19 Dance

During lockdown, a silent dance became a real treat for me. I would go to the local fields surrounded by the luxury furnished by God. His creation and colour of choice would get me moving. I would dance in silence... sometimes in fields of heather with the wind gently moving the fragrance through the air... with nobody watching but The Lord of the Silence. The emotional ring in my body wanted to scream out, but the silence of creation kept me inwardly moving in a dance.

As I beheld the splendour and solitude of God's creation, my outward dance reflected my inward awe of The Lord of the Silence, and I felt as David did in 2 Samuel 6:14, which says: "And David danced before the Lord with all his might." Unlike David, who was wearing a linen ephod, I was wearing my tracksuit with my iPhone and my headphones. That was my ephod.

Allow me to pause here for just a moment to include this note for dancers, who are so frequently connected to music. Working in silence can pose a unique challenge. Silence lays the dancer bare – and though that vulnerability is frightening, it can also be powerful.

The Beauty of Silence

I have discovered that the beauty of silence can be compared with the rotation of a diamond: the more we rotate silence, the more we realise the many ways you can experience The Lord of the Silence. Because dance is so strongly perceived as a form of communication, the silences we experience aurally also have the capacity to punctuate and illuminate communication in movement.

The point is expressing a dance in the silent earth was enriching and liberating at a time when a dance movement would appear to be very strange while people around you were dying from COVID-19. This was a personal note playing out from within a life living and enjoying the presence of God, regardless of the threats being broadcast daily gripping us silently to adjust us to a movement of stiffness and prematurely killing our joy of life. Jeremiah 31:13 says, "Then shall the young women rejoice in the dance, and the young men and the old shall be merry. I will turn their mourning into joy."

The wonder of The Lord of the Silence is that His movements are just like a dance sequence on Earth that rotate in your daily life, and the spontaneous silences and movements are tiptoeing around your routine. Sometimes we need a dance with The Lord of the silent dance for it is not the music your ears hear, but the brilliant anthems of praise that rise within, majestically silent as you respond to The Lord of the Silence with every atom of your being.

When we invite The Lord of the Silence into a turbulent situation, God promises to give us peace that "surpasses all comprehension".

Chapter 4

Peace or Panic

During this time, the topic of the coronavirus pandemic was on the lips of almost everyone around the world. The perspective for many was multifaceted: personal, economic and global, impacting millions on personal, professional and economic levels. Now, more than ever, people are searching for peace in the midst of their panic and fear-stricken lives. So many need to discover the secret of how to be still and allow God to walk into their situation.

The Reset Button

As I reflect on this time, memories come to mind of a conversation I had on a WhatsApp call with a dear friend who is a well-known author and speaker. During our chat, she told me how she had gotten so busy with ministry on line and Zoom calls (a video communications app). She said, "I'm on overload. I need some space and rest, but it's hard to find the time to do so." As she spoke, she sounded so tired and drained. She said that there were so many voices out there, but what she really needed was to hear God's voice. She went on to say, "I think I'm hearing God because I talked about reset and now everybody's talking about it. I'm so glad we're speaking, Shaneen, because you reminded me to take this time to rest and recoup to allow the reset button to be switched on personally."

My friend continued, telling me that everyone's saying the same thing. The point is, in crisis and panic we can get busier and think we're solving an issue, which may be true to a certain point. But... and this is a big 'but'... in panic, it's time to take stock and look at the virus within us, a virus addicted to busy, hurry, sin, connected to people but not God. We desire to hear His voice but His voice seems to come through louder on Twitter and other social media rather than in the silence of intimate fellowship with The Lord of the Silence.

The 'Quick Fix' Virus

The loss of personal intimacy has become an expanding gap – a virus called 'quick fix' – one that convincingly says you can't wait… viewing God through the eyes of an Amazon Prime account holder! If only God was like Amazon… a tap of the finger and what I want is on my doorstep the next morning! You undoubtedly know what I mean: thinking you've paid for a special subscription, therefore you have an entitlement to a quick fix.

Sadly, we often carry out this attitude in our spiritual lives… sometimes, unknowingly. The art of rest is lost and the heart to wait is caught up in what's next. The whole purpose for writing this book is to identify and reveal how we have lost the art of rest and the quality of life that comes from being silent and understanding the power of peace in panic. When we discover the power of that kind of peace, we become increasingly aware of the presence of God in times of darkness that cover the Earth.

Beneath the Surface

The 'perfect images' of people's perfect lives depicted on social media that surround us are most likely not what you perceive them to be. Far too many people use social media to 'live' the life they wish they had. Although COVID-19 has become a household word that has struck terror in the hearts of so many, it is invisible and only has a name. Yes, it is very serious, and if you come across it personally through symptoms or if you have already encountered it, you will know the severity of it.

Public policies and government agencies tell you that if you have any of the known symptoms, you should stay at home or ring the emergency number as so many have in the wake of this pandemic… all very serious! However, what if I were to ask if you had the symptoms of restlessness and irritability and workaholism, escapists to numbness and the fear of uncertainty? When you can't slow down, you can't focus your mind, looking for dopamine as a remedy to fix your situation. Noting all these 'symptoms', I would suggest to you that you have an interior virus of non-stop activity – a way to hide the reality or distractions such as binge-watching Netflix, browsing social media, overeating to stay alive, stressing out, afraid of being alone – behaviours that disconnect you from the real answer by stopping you from praying.

Hurry Sickness

Rushing around London was part of my daily routine although I didn't recognise it as rushing at the time. On one occasion I was due to meet a friend, Mina, for a prayer meeting. And as I was walking down the street I was frantically rushing to get there. I was in a hurry, and there was no reason to rush. Out of the blue I heard a whisper say, "I'm never in hurry." I just stood still for a moment and took in those words as if I was gasping for water, having been seized by an unquenchable thirst. This is the practice of the presence of God – simply being aware of a relationship of intimacy, an engagement that plays out daily in our lives. The dehydration of hurry robs you from being replenished by His presence. Turning this volume up helps.

Remember, God does speak to us randomly and specifically.

By simply being attentive to listen, we should expect God to speak… and it often happens when you least expect it!

Hurry kills you and you don't even realise that hurry is a threat to your spiritual well-being and spiritual life. So this pause that suddenly came upon us so dramatically with the unexpected arrival of COVID-19 prompts a question for each of us to answer personally. What can I learn from a situation like COVID-19? What will come of this awkward silence that I'm lost in? The answer: The Lord of the Silence in COVID-19 taught me personally how much I'm addicted to hurry. I have discovered anew that I don't know how to rest.

Lesson number one: you are never really prepared for crisis. COVID-19 came to the world unannounced – almost like an ambush – and pronounced in panic.

The definition of panic: sudden uncontrollable fear or anxiety, often causing wildly unthinking behaviour. But how can you think reasonably during a crisis, especially when lives are being threatened? Families and jobs at risk? How do you remain in peace?

Pause, Don't Panic

Whatever you are facing, be it a personal problem or pandemic, ask yourself, 'Is this really going to matter a year from now?' If the answer is yes, step back to remove yourself somewhat from the situation. This perspective will help you remain less emotional, rely more on reason, and allow peace – defined as freedom from disturbance; tranquillity

– to have a voice to lead your mind and heart.

Peace

The word 'peace' is used in a variety of situations ranging from a personal desire or situation in your life to the military objective of a nation. Wikipedia describes peace as a concept of societal friendship and harmony in the absence of hostility and violence. In a social sense, peace is commonly used to mean a lack of conflict (such as war) and freedom from fear of violence between individuals or groups. Throughout history, leaders have used peace-making techniques and diplomacy to establish a certain type of behavioural restraint that has resulted in the establishment of regional peace or economic growth through various forms of agreements or peace treaties. Such behavioural restraint has often resulted in the reduction of conflicts, greater economic interactivity and consequently, substantial prosperity.

On the topic of peace, Wikipedia also states "Psychological peace" (such as peaceful thinking and emotions) is perhaps less well defined, yet often a necessary precursor to establishing 'behavioural peace'. Peaceful behaviour sometimes results from a 'peaceful inner disposition'. Some have expressed the belief that peace can be initiated with a certain quality of inner tranquillity that does not depend upon the uncertainties of daily life for its existence. The acquisition of such a 'peaceful internal disposition' for oneself and others can contribute to resolving of otherwise seemingly irreconcilable competing interests (https://en.wikipedia.org/wiki/Peace).

Ultimate Peace

The peace I'm talking about is the peace of God... an effortless kind of divine tranquillity through Christ Jesus that transcends every problem, guards your heart and your thoughts, and surpasses man's ability to understand it. Perhaps you're asking, 'What's the difference? What distinguishes the peace of God from all other forms of peace?'

The Prince of Peace

Predicted and foretold by the prophet Isaiah around 700 BC, Isaiah 9:6 speaks of Jesus, referring to Him as the "Prince of Peace". I love this definition of peace: the absence of mental stress or anxiety. You may be thinking, 'What do you mean? You can actually have this kind of peace?' Most people try to achieve peace through various avenues that originate in their own abilities and techniques such as mindfulness, yoga, Buddhist philosophy and other ways outside of knowing the ancient truth about peace and from where it really originates. The prophecy quoted here by Isaiah is clearly referring to Jesus, the Prince of Peace, not panic. Later Scripture records what was written hundreds of years later in Philippians 4:6-7: "Do not be anxious about anything, but in everything by prayer and supplication with thanksgiving let your requests be made known to God. And the peace of God, which surpasses all understanding, will guard your hearts and your minds in Christ Jesus."

The Hebrew word for 'peace', shalom, is often used in reference to an appearance of calm and tranquillity of individuals, groups and nations. Paul uses eirene, a Greek word, to describe the objective of the New Testament church. But the deeper, more foundational meaning of peace is 'the spiritual harmony brought about by an individual's restoration with God'. This is the deep, abiding peace between our hearts and our Creator that cannot be taken away (John 10:27–28) and the ultimate fulfilment of Christ's work as the 'Prince of Peace', who offers the priceless gift of eternal peace.

I find it ironic that the kind of peace that is most commonly sought after – the appearance of tranquillity in an individual – is often the most difficult to obtain and maintain because it depends upon our ability to do so. In contrast, we can do absolutely nothing in our own strength or through our own abilities to acquire peace with God. The Bible says, "For by grace you have been saved through faith. And this is not your own doing; it is the gift of God, not a result of works, so that no one may boast" (Ephesians 2:8-9, ESV).

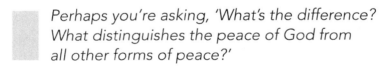

Perhaps you're asking, 'What's the difference? What distinguishes the peace of God from all other forms of peace?'

The Search For Peace

It is important to recognise that peaceful doesn't mean 'easy'. Jesus never promised that our walk with Him would be easy. In fact, He told us to expect tribulation (John 16:33) and trials (James 1:2), but He also promised to help us when He said that, if we would call on Him, He would give us the "peace of God, which surpasses all comprehension" (Philippians 4:6–7). I have found that living in unity with other Christ followers can be difficult at times. You may have experienced the same. However, living in peace in our own lives and dealing with the situations life brings our way can often seem impossible. No matter what hardships we encounter in this life, we can ask for a peace that comes from the powerful love of God that is not dependent on our own strength or any situation around us because it is a gift from God.

Peace isn't something we can achieve in our own strength. It begins when we have an encounter with Jesus, the Prince of Peace, who provides peace in the midst of every storm and crisis in life, including COVID-19. Some view this differently, but for the Christ follower, we can have peace with God and it is available to us in all circumstances. We can face scary and uncertain situations because we know that Jesus has overcome the world, and that our future is secure.

When anxious thoughts come, Scripture gives us the antidote: prayer. Some choose to regard it as meditation. Whatever your perspective, one of the greatest deceptions is to keep you busy, distracted, fill your life with noise and so much activity that there is no room for prayer, meditation or silence. If you have ever recognised that kind of thinking in yourself, pause in the midst of your busyness right now and take your panic and your fears to Jesus, the only One who can do anything about what frightens you. When we invite The Lord of the Silence into our turbulent situation, God promises to give us peace that 'surpasses all comprehension'. What a glorious exchange… our panic for His peace!

*Silence is the environment and atmosphere,
the sacred vacuum into which God speaks.*

Chapter 5

Silence Cries Out

Does silence have a voice? If so, what does it sound like? Silence responding to world events, personal heartache, crisis, an unexpected promotion, the response to a doctor's diagnosis... I believe each voice of silence in life has its own unique tone and identity. And its voice can affect one individual or the entire globe.

The Voice of Silence in History

There have been many voices of silence throughout history. For example, consider the silence that fell on the streets of New York City on 9/11. As one plane crashed into the World Trade Center, followed by the impact of another plane, thousands of confused, frightened people ran for their lives while others froze in a paralysed trance with eyes transfixed on the unfolding tragedy around them. It was a silence that started on the streets of New York City, slowly making its way across continents and around the world with the emotional force of a tsunami as the reality of what was happening unfolded on live TV.

The paralysing silence that clothed London on August 31, 1997, at the news of Princess Diana's tragic death was a stunning silence of disbelief. Referred to as the People's Princess, Diana's untimely passing brought a silent, unparalleled outpouring of love and sympathy from the citizens of England as well as from nations around the world.

When Adolf Hitler became chancellor of Germany in 1933, he stood before an expectant crowd in silence for several minutes before delivering his first speech. One minute passed, then another, as he stood with his hands folded in front of him, surveying the crowd before him standing shoulder to shoulder in a chamber of silence.

He used the power of silence to create an atmosphere of nervous energy and anticipation with the objective of drawing attention to himself. When he finally opened his mouth to speak, his words were deliberate and slow, combined with stern looks at the audience, pausing at times for emphasis. A year later he became the Führer of Germany, meaning leader or guide, a title demanded by Hitler to underscore his function as head of the Nazi Party.

Strength in Solitude

Vincent Van Gogh, a Dutch post-impressionist painter, is one of the most famous and influential figures in the history of Western art. Although his masterpieces are recognised around the world, few people are aware of the circumstances and solitude that led to his prolific career as an artist.

Born into an upper-middle-class family, Van Gogh was a quiet, thoughtful child. As a young man Vincent turned to religion and spent time as a Protestant missionary. When he sought to become a pastor just like his father before him, he was rejected by a theological college and also the Church. His love of Christ led him to imitate Him and extend his helping hand to the poor and others. The Church found him to be overzealous, described as excès de zèle.

The Silent Artist

Rejected by the Church, his younger brother Theo, an art dealer in Paris, encouraged him to take up art and funded his existence and his work. In just over a decade, Van Gogh created over 2,000 pieces of artwork, including around 860 oil paintings, most of them in the last two years of his life. His early work focused on still lives and peasant workers, void of the vivid colour that distinguished his later work. As his work advanced, he took a new approach with his artwork, using bold colours in his landscapes, still lives, portraits and self-portraits, and are recognised by the dramatic, expressive brushwork that was foundational to modern art. Despite the volume of pieces he produced, very few sold, and those that sold brought in very little money.

During this time of Van Gogh's life, Theo continued looking after his elder brother. Vincent was overzealous in all that he turned his hand and mind to. Drinking, womanising, bouts of bipolar episodes and frenetic artwork, Vincent's mind eventually overtook him and he famously cut off part of his ear followed by suicide from pistol wounds. Vincent was 37 years of age when he died, and nine months after his death, his brother Theo died at age 33.

Theo's young widow was aware of the works and maintained the collection in its entirety. Today, 125 years on, these works are in museums, galleries and private collections throughout the world. Sold and valued for hundreds of millions of dollars, the unpaid artist's works over nine years prove the genius of Van Gogh.

The Greatest Artist

Even though the Church in their judgemental humanity rejected Vincent, The Lord of the Silence did not, and through that silent gift bestowed upon his hands and eyes, some of the finest paintings of God's creation were realised. From sunflowers, wheat fields and trees, The Lord of the Silence is seen in each painting. The Sower, painted in 1888, reminds us of the parable and how some seed falls on stony ground while others bloom. Though some seeds are rejected, The Lord of the Silence still uses them and in doing so, creates from life's plain canvas a full and complete painting of our lives, valued by others, loved by some and eternally speaking.

The Silence of Life

Silence can be intimidating on a personal level, especially when it is related to personal experiences. It has no regard for age, affecting young and old alike. For example, as a child were you ever subjected to the 'wait' outside the headmaster's office that seemed to last an eternity, waiting in the silence as if you were invisible? Perhaps you have found yourself waiting nervously for medical test results or a diagnosis in the cold, sterile environment of a physician's examination room.

The silence of fear may have even come knocking at your door. Similar feelings of apprehension can arise in a courtroom as silence blankets the room while the destiny of an individual hangs in the balance.

The parameters of silence are almost immeasurable. The voice of silence cries out in all kinds of settings in life, including relationships. Have you ever experienced the uncomfortable silence on a first date, or the threatening silence used by couples in a dispute? Even as an onlooker seated at a nearby table in an exquisite restaurant, the voice of silence draws you into the couple's first date or the couple's disagreement as you sense the tension in the air.

During World War I, trench warfare was used by the forces who mounted attacks with bayonets on their rifles as they climbed out of the trenches into 'no man's land', the area between them and their enemy. During the Battle of the Somme in France in 1916, the British troops suffered 60,000 casualties on the very first day. Conditions in the trenches were horrific due to the presence of corpses, rats, infectious diseases and unsanitary conditions. Yet, there was often a peaceful silence just ahead of the outbreak of death and destruction.

47 Minutes of Silence

Half a century ago, Neil Armstrong and Buzz Aldrin were part of the historic first manned mission known as Apollo 11 to land on the moon. Armstrong and Aldrin were the first humans to step onto the surface of the moon and made themselves household names because much is always spoken of them both. The third astronaut on that Apollo 11 mission – not as well known – was Michael Collins who remained inside the command module throughout the mission.

As part of the crew, Collins' achievement was equal to that of Armstrong and Aldrin. Yet, his experience was unique because he was separated from contact with any one of the 3 billion people on Earth and the two men on the moon as he orbited the dark side of the moon. Collins flew the command module Columbia alone in lunar orbit while Armstrong and Aldrin were on the moon's surface. The two men spent 21 hours and 36 minutes on the moon while Collins, aboard Columbia, orbited the moon 30 times. During each of the 30 orbits, Collins, often the forgotten astronaut on Apollo 11, encountered 47 minutes of sinister silence on the dark side of the moon with no radio contact and absolute silence.

2,820 Seconds

Consider how long 47 minutes of silence is by taking a moment for this experiment. Find a dark place and be silent and still for 60 seconds. Just let the seconds tick by... one by one... tick... tick... tick! As you reached that milestone of one minute of silence, did that seem like a long time? Now try to comprehend how long 2,820 seconds is, which equals 47 minutes. That's what Michael Collins experienced every time he orbited the dark side of the moon during Armstrong and Aldrin's 21 hours and 36 minutes on the moon's surface!

The Apollo command module with Collins aboard remained in orbit just 60 miles above the moon while Armstrong stepped onto the moon's surface and uttered the words that would be recorded in history books for generations to come: "That's one small step for man; one giant leap for mankind." While half a billion people on Earth watched and celebrated this historic event, Michael Collins was above the far side of the moon, cut off from all communication – alone in the silence.

Collins said later that he had his fears with him; fears that something would go wrong with the command module Columbia or that the lunar ascent module would fail, leaving both men stranded on the moon and him having to return home as the lucky-to-survive one. Collins had to overcome these fears several times... alone... immersed in 47 minutes of silence.

In our own lives, we too travel through dark-sided times gripped by fears that go off at tangent trauma. We often go through such episodes in silence and, though surrounded now by 7.5 billion people on Earth and currently no one on the moon, it can be sinister. In these times, outcomes are unknown though one thing is certain that such a time will pass. And into the light you will emerge with another life experience that prepares you for life's journey and the realisation that in this time, The Lord of the Silence is still looking out for you.

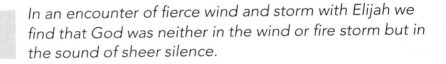

In an encounter of fierce wind and storm with Elijah we find that God was neither in the wind or fire storm but in the sound of sheer silence.

All these voices of silence reveal different emotions in a voice of uncertainty as to what the outcome might be. However, the silence I am speaking of is different. It is the place where striving ends and a place of rest is found. It is an established location of calm and stillness... a place where panic does not exist, but where the presence of peace without murmuring flourishes.

In The Stillness

I believe silence is heard. You may ask, 'How can one hear a nothing though?' My response is that silence must speak for itself, and we can find a number of examples throughout Scripture.

In the beginning we read in Genesis that there was absolute silence. Into that silence God spoke His word and the heavens and the Earth were created. God speaks out of silence to bring all things into existence by the power of His creative word. This creativity has continued throughout history, and both word and silence complement each other.

Silence, God's Sacred Vacuum

Silence is the environment and atmosphere, that sacred vacuum into which God speaks. In the Old Testament we see silence becoming the medium for divine revelation. In an encounter of fierce wind and storm with Elijah we find that God was neither in the wind or fire storm but in the sound of sheer silence. In that place, God reveals His presence and purpose.

The Land of Silence

Later scholars perceived silence in a negative way as the land of silence became Sheol, the place of the dead and was regarded as a place where God was not found. This view was exacerbated in Isaiah 47:5 which declares, "Sit in silence and go into darkness, daughter Chaldea." Silence was darkness and darkness is death. The Psalmist, however, led us in a different direction when in Psalm 4:4 he urges the sinner to "commune with your own hearts on your bed and be silent."

The prophet Zephaniah reminded the people, "Be silent for the day of The Lord is at hand" (Zephaniah 1:7). The day of The Lord is an end times day of judgement, a day of vindication, blessing and the bestowal of everlasting peace. These qualities are both given and received in silence.

Hearing God's Voice

Meantime, Israel perceived the silence of the prophets to be a sign of God's judgement though the less paranoid early Christians saw the silence as new creation and revelation. The coming of Jesus Christ brings the new creation of the Church, the universal body of Christ. Through His coming, the heart can now attain the gift of silence where we can find stillness, enabling us to listen to the voice of God and hear The Lord of the Silence.

In the New Testament, little is said of silence, though we see Christ with the ability to silence His adversaries and to still the storms upon the waters through His rebuke (Mark 4:39). Jesus spoke to the storm and the wind and the waves were stilled. We see through the life and ministry of Jesus that whether it is the human heart or the open seas, peace requires stillness. In the midst of our own storms and turmoil Jesus speaks those same words to us today, "Peace, be still."

"

We must silence the noise of society that surrounds us to know The Lord of the Silence.

Chapter 6

Sacred Place of Silence

If you have attended church, perhaps you've heard an occasional reference to 'God's presence' or 'the presence of God'. But what does that phrase really mean? You may sing songs about God's presence on Sunday morning when you gather at your place of worship as I do, or you may hear the term in a sermon from time to time. But, in the end, do we really understand what God's presence is or how we can experience it on a personal level?

What Is God's Presence?

God is omnipresent, which means He is present in all places all the time. In the beginning, Adam and Eve experienced the joy of God's presence with them in the Garden of Eve before they sinned. But after they sinned, they became separated from His presence, choosing to hide from Him. "And they heard the sound of the Lord God walking in the garden in the cool of the day, and the man and his wife hid themselves from the presence of the Lord God among the trees of the garden" (Genesis 3:8).

Today, God's presence dwells with those who believe in Him (John 14:23). God is present at all times in all places and in each believer. We do not need to go to a special place or location to find His presence. Rather, we can experience His presence through worship, meditation or prayer, which comes from our hearts. It can happen anywhere because God is omnipresent so it can happen anywhere because it is a lifestyle!

God's presence can be experienced personally throughout the day. Often we put God in a box and expect to experience Him in a certain environment such as Sunday morning as we sit in the church pew or at a conference, a prayer meeting or in a building. All of these are good, yet His presence is not confined to any of these places. To really enjoy a relationship, you must have a desire to get to know the person through time and awareness of their presence. Imagine being in the same room with your spouse or friend and being unaware that they are there. How would you feel if someone you care about behaved in such a manner? If you care that deeply about someone who is just flesh and blood as you are, how much more about God Almighty, the Creator of heaven and Earth!

Experiencing God's Presence

The presence of God is real and you can experience it. God's presence is not limited to any set pattern regarding how you and I can recognise His presence. I have found that there are times when you hear a gentle whisper. One of my experiences of this was when I returned from my church in London, from a service for pastorate leaders to be trained to lead small home groups in the church. My husband was super excited about this and I was not. My lack of excitement was based on the fact that I didn't really want to be a public leader at that time, especially as I was a youth pastor for many years and felt that after going through a divorce, I would never return to public ministry. Added to my own apprehension was the fact that some churchgoers can be very judgemental, so I had decided to put a pause on any kind of involvement in public ministry.

An Unexpected Encounter

During the night I heard a whisper to turn the TV on. I thought, "That can't be the Holy Spirit; He normally tells me to switch it off." Again I heard His voice. This time I decided to switch the television on with a loud sigh. As the TV came on, a man named Steve Hill was speaking – and it seemed that he was speaking to me! His words drew me in immediately as he said, "There's a woman in London... I'm speaking to you. You're divorced and you're running away from ministry. God is calling you back. Repent and watch how God is going to use you and restore you." As he spoke, the presence of God gushed into my room with a stillness that awakened me, a silence that stirred me to respond to the call. In the silence of the night hours, I waited as the presence of God rested on me. An indescribable peace that flowed from my innermost bought me to a place of what I call a turnaround moment. It was almost like saying, "Hi God. Wow! You never give up on us, no matter how low we feel or fall. You speak to us in the most unusual ways."

It was about 3 am, and I decided to go upstairs to share what was happening with my husband, Martin. When I reached the bedroom, I found him snug in bed. I tapped him gently on the shoulder and said, "Can you feel Him?" Trying to rouse himself from his sleep and not fully awake, Martin said, "Feel what?" "His presence," I responded. Opening his sleepy eyes a little wider, Martin replied, "What do you mean?" I explained what had happened moments before. When I finished speaking, Martin said, "I can't feel Him like you do," and with that, he popped back into bed.

I went downstairs to linger in the euphoric atmosphere that I had experienced earlier. It was a place unlike anything I had ever felt before. It may sound a bit odd, but it's as real to me as I write this book as it was at 3 am that morning when it happened. In that moment I enjoyed what can only be described as a secret silence for three hours. During those hours, my heart understood what King David talked about when he said, "Your presence is all I need."

I totally understand what David was speaking about in Psalms about God's presence. I realised I was undone just as David had said of himself. Immersed in that secret silence for three hours, I was removing all the limits I had about God and His dwelling place as spoken of in Psalm 91, which says, "He that dwelleth in the secret place of the most High shall abide under the shadow of the Most High." Since that experience in the secret silence, this is a reality that has changed my life and ministry.

Today so many are in search for a higher power – a force or a power –

that's beyond the human nature. The presence of God is not an 'it', a 'thing', or energy. It is a person and this person has feelings, a mind, and He can touch you right where you hurt. In those soft spots, in places where you have been wounded. Yes, it's called the power of God's presence. It's real, it's powerful, it's engaging, and it's with you as you read this book. Don't be afraid of His presence. People go to all sorts of places to have an experience or an encounter, but you can have this right where you are.

It's real, it's powerful, it's engaging, and it's with you as you read this book.

Relationship vs Religion

Over the years I've learnt that I don't have to just wait for a feeling or a tingling sensation as some might desire. The presence of God is not some weird, wacky feeling. It's beyond that. I write this from a life of living out this reality from a place of union with His presence. I hear of people who are bored with life religion and I understand their viewpoint. You would be bored if you don't take the time to just shut up and stand up to the noise that surrounds you daily, drowning you in fear, doubt and restlessness. Yes, I'm inviting you to take the next step to spend time to get to know Him… not the philosophy, science and theology but the God who met Israel at Sinai. Jesus is not an imaginary figure. He was more than just a spiritual man. Scepticism abandons all idea of this. Knowing about the God whose world it is and runs it is only part of the experience. Knowing about God is crucial but knowing Him personally is life changing and transforming.

Getting Started

How are we to do this? If we turn each truth that we learn about God into a matter for meditation before God, it will lead to prayer and waiting on Him.

Charles Spurgeon, often referred to as the 'Prince of preachers', understood these principles. Regarded as the most extraordinary preacher of his day and England's best- known for most of the second half of the 19th century, he said the following, speaking about the place of silence in our walk with God: "There are times when solitude is better than society, and silence is wiser than speech. We should be better Christians if we were more alone, waiting upon God, and gathering through meditation on His Word spiritual strength for labour in his service."

In my opinion, meditation is a lost art today and we suffer grievously from ignorance of the practice. In his book titled Knowing God, J. I. Packer says, "Meditation is the activity of calling to mind, and thinking over, and dwelling on, and applying to one's self the various things that one knows about the works and ways and purposes and promises of God. It is an activity of holy thought, consciously performed in the presence of God, by the help of God, as a means of communication with God."

Andrew Murray shared this nugget of wisdom when he said, "A soul cannot seek close fellowship with God, or attain the abiding consciousness of waiting on Him all the day, without a very honest and entire surrender to all His will." If you and I want to know God, we must allow ourselves to go deeper and pursue Him with our hearts as we would pursue a person we want to know on a more intimate level. To have a clearer understanding of God's presence, I believe we must silence the noise of society that surrounds us in order to know The Lord of the Silence. Today, the modern man wants to be entertained or amused, which is the opposite of muse (another word for meditation). Noise and entertainment are the natural weapons of the chaotic world in which we live that distract us and stop us from communing with God in a sanctuary of silence. When we embrace silence and prepare our hearts in stillness, we close the door of distraction to allow our hearts to meditate upon who God is as David observed in Psalm 46:10: "Be still and know that I am God." In that silence we begin to hear God speaking to us, calling us to Him as our earthly, natural-minded thoughts fade, giving way to meditating on His greatness and the truth of His word. The more we meditate upon God, the more intimate our relationship with Him grows.

A Lifestyle In God's Presence

Nicholas Herman, also known through his writings as Brother Lawrence, understood how to live in God's presence. Born around 1610, he was a man of humble beginnings. Educated from an early age by a parish priest whose first name was Lawrence, Nicholas came to admire him very much.

Nicholas was well read and longed to live a spiritual life of faith and love for God. Wounded as a young soldier and sustaining near-fatal injuries, he was crippled and suffered with chronic pain for most of his adult life. With the limitations of his injuries, he entered a monastery and joined the Order of Discalced Carmelites in Paris at age 24, taking the religious name 'Lawrence of the Resurrection'. For the next 40 years, Brother Lawrence served in various capacities including in the kitchen and sandal repair. It was during this time that he discovered the secret of how to live a lifestyle continually in God's presence. During the course of his service at the parish, he wrote a number of letters about the practice of God's presence. Only after his death were some of his letters discovered and published under the title, The Practice of the Presence of God.

A book small in size but rich in content, The Practice of the Presence of God includes 15 short letters penned by Brother Lawrence to long-time friends during the last ten years of his life. It is a small book but rich in content, explaining in simple terms how to walk with God and live in His presence as a lifestyle. It begins with his reflections on his conversion to a deeper commitment to his Christian faith at age 18 and focuses on the lifestyle of living in God's presence. He said, "After having given myself wholly to God, to make all the satisfaction I could for my sins, I renounced, for the love of Him, everything that was not He, and I began to live as if there was none but He and I in the world."

There are special effects in our lives related to knowing God. Undoubtedly, you know what it's like watching a movie with special effects. That's what it's like watching a person who knows their God (Daniel 11:32). Meditating upon God's character and greatness, listening in silence as God speaks to us, and contemplating the truth He whispers to our hearts is an experience so humbling it is difficult to describe in mere words. Created from a piece of dust into whom He breathed the breath of life as He created us in His image, we can walk and talk with Him each day, experiencing His presence and all that it brings to our lives.

When our minds and hearts understand that a lifestyle wrapped in God's presence is possible, our hearts will begin to beat with the burning desire that Brother Lawrence experienced and wrote about. And in that moment of awareness, we will pray the prayer that Andrew Murray prayed: "May not a single moment of my life be spent outside the light, love, and joy of God's presence."

As your inner longing intensifies to know The Lord of the Silence more intimately, shut out the noise of the world around you and the distracting thoughts that are continually rushing through your mind. Find a quiet place where you can be still; a place where you can hear His gentle, loving voice calling you to Him. And as God's indescribable presence wraps you and becomes more real to you than life itself, you will walk with Him in stillness just as Adam and Eve did in the Garden of Eden as The Lord of the Silence shines His love upon you.

Sometimes to enjoy God is to know rest.
Rest is best in the presence of God.

Chapter 7

Understanding The Lord of the Silence

Growing up in London, my pastor, who was a Scottish revivalist in the Assembly of God church, would often talk about a woman named Kathryn Kuhlman, an American evangelist from German roots, who was known for her healing meetings. He recalled being there as an usher among so many others from across the States and talked about the people who would travel for days for the sole purpose of being in her meetings. On the day the meeting was to take place, thousands would wait for hours outside the building, unaffected by the chilling winter winds or falling snow, anticipating the moment when the doors would open for them to enter so they could attend a Kathryn Kuhlman meeting.

When the doors would finally swing open, those who had been lined up outside the building would rush in to find a seat as close to the front as possible where they waited patiently for the meeting to begin. I have heard that upon entering the building, the atmosphere was charged with an invisible power and presence that seemed almost tangible. While thousands waited in anticipation in that atmosphere, the minutes ticked by as the auditorium filled to capacity, and it was finally time for the meeting to begin. As the lights dimmed and the music started to play, a spotlight welcomed a red-haired, tall, slender woman with a unique voice – wonderfully put together by God.

One of the stories my pastor shared about her held me spellbound initially and ultimately made my hair stand up. He said that on one occasion as thousands waited for the spotlight to light the path for her entrance, as expected, she walked onto the stage, dressed in her floor-length, flowing gown. But then the unexpected happened as she suddenly stopped where she was standing and began to sob uncontrollably. This behaviour on the part of Ms Kuhlman caught everyone by surprise and temporarily stopped the meeting! When she finally regained her composure on some level, she just stood there, elegantly posed, looking at the audience. Then she said with a loud cry, "He's all I've got! He's all I've got!" If you weren't a Christian, perhaps you would have thought she had lost the plot. But that was not the case, for she was uttering words to the Holy Spirit. As the audience watched in silence, Kathryn turned and pointed her long finger towards someone and said with a slow, deliberate cadence, "You're grieving the Holy Spirit!" As she said the words "The Holy Spirit" the words left her lips in slow motion, almost as if she was exhaling. As she spoke the words, there was pin-drop silence along with a wow factor... you know, the wow of God when His presence is there, and you sense you can't say a word, knowing the silence speaks for itself. Suddenly, her slowly articulated words turned to an authoritative command as she said to the person, "Receive your healing!" The woman she was pointing at was crying as Kathryn Kuhlman spoke, and she received her healing.

Most young people today have never heard of her, nor have they seen the kinds of miracles that took place in Ms Kuhlman's services. Equally tragic, these same youth have not experienced that level of God's power.

Silence and Sensitivity

The point I want to make relates to her remarkable sensitivity to the presence of God. This is what I call being sensitive to the presence. When was the last time you witnessed such sensitivity? Often her meetings would have a pause of silence, and in those moments, the atmosphere intensified and changed. Sometimes we can get accustomed to noise, even equating it with spirituality. We often pick up beliefs that power is only in noise, but it's not true.

Pentecostals are known for noise. I grew up as one, but now I attend an evangelical church in London. It has Anglican roots, so I call myself a refined Pentecostal. I have learnt that you don't have to work up the presence of God, making lots of effort to see if His presence shows up. You just need to know His presence, which comes as you desire His presence and become acquainted with His presence.

In the early 90s, a friend of mine who was a full-blown Pentecostal pastor from the north of England came to visit our church, which at the time was having an awakening or a revival in Central London. Hundreds came to see and witness what was happening. John Wimber was instrumental and used mighty by God to stir this movement among the Anglican Church in the gifts of healing and word of knowledge.

Well, this pastor friend of mine who was a Pentecostal came and joined some English ladies in 'the spring' room in our church, which is a place set aside for prayer. "Well," he thought, "I wonder what these quiet Anglicans could teach us Pentecostals. We know all about the power of the Holy Spirit and speaking in tongues." As he stood waiting to be prayed for, a very tall English lady laid her hands upon him, and very gently began to pray, saying, "Come, Holy Spirit," which also happens to be the shortest prayer in the Bible. My friend thought, "That kind of prayer is not going to do anything." Once again, she prayed in similar fashion. Standing there with a long flowing skirt, she said again with a gentle whisper, "Come Holy Spirit." As she prayed quietly, waiting for the presence of God to touch my friend, my friend was thinking, "A little louder, please; come on." But there was silence in the room. Then suddenly he got hit by the power of God and couldn't stop laughing, dancing, and was filled with the Spirit which he recalls lasted all day. They had to carry him to the car park and then home. He was later used by God in the north of England powerfully, having received the prayer from an Anglican church in London. He took the revival prayer back, and he too experienced the revival breaking out for a number of years in the north of England.

The Spirit Works In Stillness

You see, power is not found in noise or methods or formulas. It's not contingent on rituals or traditions. The Holy Spirit works in stillness, and in noise, He has many ways in which He manifests His power and presence. But let's not limit the power of quietness or stillness. In quietness and stillness, we shall find rest. "For thus saith the Lord GOD, the Holy One of Israel; In returning and rest shall ye be saved; in quietness and confidence shall be your strength: and ye would not" (Isaiah 30:15).

Sometimes to enjoy God is to know rest. Rest is best in the presence of God. There is a time to shout, a time to scream the house down, make a shout to the Lord, and make a noise. But I am encouraging you to invest in stillness.

Peace in The Storm

The songwriter, Horatio Gates Spafford, is best known for penning the Christian hymn titled 'It Is Well With My Soul'. Before he ever wrote the words of this classic hymn, scarlet fever took his young son from him. Two years later, in 1873, Spafford decided his family should take a holiday somewhere in Europe. He chose England, knowing that his friend, D. L. Moody would be preaching there in the fall. Prior to the holiday, Spafford was delayed because of business. He decided to send his family, which included his wife and four daughters: 11-year-old Anna 'Annie', nine-year-old Margaret Lee 'Maggie', five-year-old Elizabeth 'Bessie', and two-year-old Tanetta.

The Place of Rest

On November 22, 1873, while crossing the Atlantic on the steamship Ville du Havre, their ship was struck by an iron sailing vessel, and 226 people lost their lives, including all four of Spafford's daughters. His wife Anna Spafford survived the tragedy. Upon arriving in England, she sent a telegram to Spafford beginning with the words, "Saved alone." Spafford then sailed to England, going over the location of his daughters' deaths. According to Bertha Spafford Vester, a daughter born after the tragedy, Spafford wrote the hymn, 'It Is Well with My Soul', on this journey.

The lyrics of the song's first stanza reflect the depths of the writer's heartache following a family tragedy in which his four daughters died aboard the S.S. Ville du Havre on a transatlantic voyage:

When peace like a river attendeth my way,
When sorrows like sea billows roll.
Whatever my lot, thou hast taught me to say
It is well; it is well, with my soul.

With the exception of his wife, Horatio Gates Spafford lost his entire family and was still able to sing and write a song of peace like a river, which is what God's presence does. In the midst of your noisy, painful life – or in the course of your not-so-painful but unfulfilling life – God is waiting to be your peace and still your storm-tossed life.

Learning to Rest

My friend, it is well with your soul. You don't have to strive in the presence. Learning just to be and do nothing brings out songs, ideas and revelation, and vision, pictures to impressions and dreams. God wants you to rest and just be. Allow your sensitivity to develop just like Kathryn Kuhlman when she knew someone hurt her only love, the Holy Spirit. There is a place like a river that touches every part of your being. It is my prayer that you learn and desire to have a sensitive heart towards His presence and that even though you may be going through a difficult patch in your life, you too can write a song and have an idea, a vision, a plan that can only be downloaded when at rest.

When we try to do everything in our own strength and leave God out of the equation, we get worn out, troubled and frustrated by our mistakes and our failures. But when we lean on God's presence, we actually enter into His rest and can enjoy our lives, no matter what our circumstances may be. When you find yourself getting frustrated or feeling overwhelmed, saying you can't do it anymore, remember to stop and get your focus back on Him as you enter into His rest.

The Rest of God

Now the rest of God is not a rest from work – it's a rest in work. It's partnering with God to do what He is calling you to do by His grace, and leaving the part you can't do in His hands, trusting Him to do it. Hebrews 4:3 says it this way: "For we who have believed (adhered to and trusted in and relied on God) do enter that rest." We start by believing and becoming more and more tuned into His presence daily in our lives and the lives of others.

How can you find rest and renewal in the midst of your hectic life? Simply become very aware of God's presence, realising that He will help you with your responsibilities. "Come to me, all you who are weary and burdened, and I will give you rest. Take my yoke upon you and learn from me, for I am gentle and humble in heart, and you will find rest for your souls" (Matthew 11:28-29). God will show you how to work with the conservation of energy, how to work in a relaxed manner, and feel rested rather than tired.

The next time you're feeling tired, struggling with your workload or your worries, say this verse aloud several times: "My presence will go with you, and I will give you rest" (Exodus 33:14). Personalise the scripture by inserting your name wherever the word 'you' appears. For example, 'My presence will go with Shaneen, and I will give Shaneen rest.' Meditate on these life-changing words: I WILL GIVE YOU REST – the very words every tired soul longs to hear!

"

*The harder our toil, the more let us see to it
that we keep a little cell within the central life
where in silence we hold communion with
The Lord of the Silence.*

Chapter 8

Silent Refuge

While writing this book I had laryngitis (a vocal box problem) for six weeks and was advised by my doctor not to talk too much. You know women love to chat and when told to talk less, it's a challenge. As English newspaper Daily Mail noted, "Sorry to interrupt, dear, but women really do talk more than men – 13,000 words a day more to be precise."

Marinated in Quietness

During my six weeks of silence, I had to learn to pray without speaking or using my voice, and believe me, it was difficult, laborious, and tough as you can get. Worse than having a baby… okay, that might be a bit far-fetched. Describing it as a peculiar feeling may be more accurate because I was used to praying aloud. There have been times I've prayed silently and enjoyed being in the presence of stillness while trying to get God's attention through words or praise.

Simply being myself and letting go of the religious side of prayer and duty in those moments of silence is somewhat like having a relationship with someone you've known for a while. You feel so comfortable in their presence and don't feel like you have to walk on eggshells to be understood. There's no need for filtering your words of communication because you know them so your approach is just being. This is what I loved about these times of not speaking in prayer but praying from the heart. In light of the laryngitis, my throat was very sore and hurt; it was good to take the option to just be quiet.

A Lesson Behind the Silence

So what did I learn? That you don't need your voice to communicate. You can communicate with God without speaking a word audibly and feel the depth of your prayers and His presence. In the end, my 'six-weeks of-silence' experience took me deeper and I developed a sense of the 'wow factor' of His presence to be enjoyed as well as the realisation of how much we miss out on related to the quality of quiet prayer.

During these times of silent refuge, I would get pictures, ideas and a revelation of the power of allowing myself to enter into a position of oneness with The Lord of the Silence. As I studied the Scriptures on this subject, John 15:5 stood out to me and brought such revelation to my soul.

"I am the vine; you are the branches. If you remain in me and I in you, you will bear much fruit; apart from me you can do nothing" (John 15:5, NIV). The message translation added to my understanding:

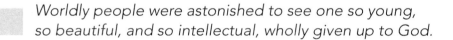
Worldly people were astonished to see one so young, so beautiful, and so intellectual, wholly given up to God.

"I am the Vine, you are the branches. When you're joined with me and I with you, the relation intimate and organic, the harvest is sure to be abundant. Separated, you can't produce a thing. Anyone who separates from me is deadwood, gathered up and thrown on the bonfire. But if you make yourselves at home with me and my words are at home in you, you can be sure that whatever you ask will be listened to and acted upon. This is how my Father shows who he is – when you produce grapes, when you mature as my disciples" (John 15:5-8, MSG).

The Secret Place

I began to understand my need to get away into the 'secret place of the Most High', and rise into a higher altitude and atmosphere rather than remain in the region of work and effort. I recognised the importance of sitting still with Christ to allow His love and His power to pour into my heart. "Come, My people, enter thou into thy chambers and shut thy doors about thee" (Isaiah 26:20). It was a wonderful experience and I encourage you to do the same. Get away from the jangling of politics, empty controversies and busy distractions of your daily duties. The harder our toil necessarily is, the more let us see to it that we keep a little cell within the central life where in silence we hold communion with the Master. "Abide in Me and I in you" (John 15:4).

A Dynamic Example

Communing with God through silence, in many instances, deepens through understanding and repetition. An example from church history of one who discovered this place of refuge through silent communion with God is Mademoiselle De La Mothe, or Madame Jeanne Guyon, as she came to be known. She is admired by many, including John Wesley who said of her, "How few such instances do we find of exalted love to God, and our neighbour; of genuine humility; of invincible meekness and unbounded resignation." Not everyone would agree with Wesley, however. The Roman Catholic Church of 17th-century France, in which she grew up, burned her books, condemned her principles of Quietism, and imprisoned her. What was it about this woman of God that brought such varied reactions?

Madame Jeanne Guyon

Her journey began when she was living in fashionable Paris as a young girl, in the times of Louis XIV, a ruler who was perhaps the most pleasure-loving, corrupt and dissolute who ever cursed the sunny land of France. At the time, it was very easy for her to be carried away by the worldliness around her. Her talents and her beauty made her highly susceptible to the influences of the fashionable society.

A product of French high society, Jeanne was raised in convents from the age of two and a half. Her parents belonged to the aristocracy of France, were highly respected and were religiously inclined as were their forefathers for many generations. At ten years old, she found a Bible left in her room and began earnestly to study and memorise it. From then on, she pursued an exclusive devotion to God. Prayer was the greatest pleasure of her life. Worldly people were astonished to see one so young, so beautiful, and so intellectual, wholly given up to God. Pleasure-loving society felt condemned by her life and sought to persecute and ridicule her.

In 1664, at 15 years of age, after turning down many other proposals, she was forced into an arranged marriage to a wealthy gentleman named Jacques Guyon, a 38-year-old man. During her 12 years of marriage, Guyon suffered terribly at the hands of her mother-in-law and maidservant. Adding to her misery were the deaths of her half-sister, followed by her mother and her son. Her daughter and father then died within days of each other in July 1672. Guyon continued her belief in God's perfect plan, trusting that she would be blessed in suffering. To this end she was indeed blessed, when she bore another son and daughter shortly before her husband's death in 1676. After 12 years of an unhappy marriage (in which she had borne five children, of whom three had survived), Madame Guyon became a widow at the age of 28.

As she wrote in one of her poems: "There was a period when I chose, A time and place for prayer... But now I seek that constant prayer, In inward stillness known..."

A Heart After God

The Roman Catholic Church at that time opposed what they referred to as her Quietism, which teaches that spiritual perfection can be attained when self is lost in the contemplation of God. The authorities also warned her that it was the business of priests to pray, not women, and certainly not in the way she prayed – with intimacy, from her heart. Unmoved by intimidation and popular among all levels of society, she fearlessly used every chance to share her spiritual ideas with everyone she encountered.

Known to be a French mystic, she was accused of advocating Quietism, a doctrine of Christian spirituality that, in general, holds that perfection consists of passivity (quiet) of the soul, in the suppression of human effort so that divine action may have full play. Although she never called herself a Quietist, Quietism was considered heretical by the Roman Catholic Church, and she was imprisoned from 1695 to 1703 after publishing the book, A Short and Easy Method of Prayer. The church finally had her arrested and sent to prison for eight years, spending the last two in solitary confinement in the Bastille. She continued to write, having produced a 20-volume commentary on the Bible, an autobiography (available at the Christian Classics Ethereal Library), and many short works, two of which can be accessed at Dialogues and Documents from the Past: "The Way to God: and of the State of Union".

In 1709, after her release from prison, Madame Guyon wrote a retrospective account of her nearly eight years of incarceration which spanned the years of 1695–1703. The thoughts she shared were intended for private distribution to her closest friends, and were thought to have been lost to history, perhaps destroyed by Louis XIV or his agents in the prison hierarchy or by the church itself. Although her earlier Life would be published many times and become a crucial text for her mystical spirituality, the prison account remained unknown until the late 1980s, when Marie-Louise Gondal discovered a handwritten copy in the Jesuit Library in Chantilly.

Gondal published the text in French in 1992 as Récits de captivité, inédit: autobiographie, quatrième partie.

After King Louis XIV released her from prison, Madame Guyon lived another 15 years, suffering patiently and glorifying God in her illnesses until she died at age 69.

Silence in Death

Some find silent refuge in life as Madame Jeanne Guyon did. Others discover the refuge of silence in death. I experienced this facet of silence personally in March 2004 with my mother-in-law who had been diagnosed with terminal breast cancer and given three months to live. Her husband of over 55 years and her three siblings along with many friends and family were distraught. Though she was 78 years of age, she had been a stalwart of the family and was much loved by all.

On Friday, June 18th, she was admitted into the palliative care unit of a Surrey hospital and went into a deep coma with all her loved ones gathered around her bed. The family kept vigil for the next 48 hours, and though it is said that those in a coma can hear but not respond, we will never know if that is true.

At around 4 pm on that Sunday afternoon as we stood at her bedside, her eyes opened as she shot up from the bed with arms raised and the broadest of smiles you could ever imagine poised on her lips. With her arms outstretched and in light of the sudden change in the atmosphere in that room, Mary Patricia was being taken home by either a legion of angels or Christ himself. Completely oblivious to all of us in the room at that moment, her tears ran down the side of her cheek, though we now know that they were tears of joy. All in shock, we watched her body peacefully lay back on the bed and it was as plain as day, she was no longer there. It was the end of this life and the beginning of the next.

Slipping Away in Silence

It was the most beautiful of scenes, and within minutes the doctor appeared to pronounce death and as she did that, the most wonderful of rainbows appeared outside the window of the hospital room. Within the room there was a deathly silence with her spirit gone. The absence of all sound was almost deafening as the reality of what had just transpired gripped the hearts of those present in the room. As her lifeless body lay there, and though stricken with grief at her passing, we thanked The Lord of the Silence for coming to take her home with such a glorious departure from this earth – into eternity, His bosom and the place that He had prepared for her.

It was a moment of great grief, yet great hope; great sadness, yet great encouragement and a gift to have been present to witness her departure from this life into eternity.

The words of the Psalmist David declare, "God is our refuge and strength, a very present help in trouble" (Psalm 46:1). Whether in life as Madame Jeanne Guyon experienced, or at the passing of a loved one, The Lord of the Silence is our refuge.

Being silent is like strong medicine that heals us, transforms us, and makes space for a deeper engagement with God and others.

Chapter 9

Healing Silence

Travelling these days is not as glamorous as it once was. The entire experience of going anywhere for either business or pleasure is more complicated and is often preceded by so many obstacles — like going through security at an airport and being scanned while walking into and pausing momentarily as a machine scans you from head to toe. Then as you exit the machine, you encounter a stern-faced official staring at you as if you're in trouble. At times the alarm goes off and the security officer asks you to step aside to see if you're hiding something questionable. As you watch your carry-on or your handbag move down the conveyor after being scanned, you're thinking, "Go ahead and search me if you will; I don't have anything to hide."

In response to the alarm, airport security reaches for a slender pole, attaching some kind of small fabric swatch on the end before swabbing your hands or an item in your bag. While the computer runs an analysis on the fabric swatch, you are asked to step aside and wait. When the process is complete and nothing questionable is found, the security officer turns to you and says, "Okay, have a nice day." Whether something like this happens before your departure or at customs after returning from an international destination, the experience is almost always unsettling to say the least.

I've encountered this situation a number of times, but when it happens to your 82-year-old mother, it is an entirely different experience on another level. On one of her visits, I was standing outside the security doors as my mother was about to exit after clearing customs. I had only been waiting a few minutes when I heard all the alarms going off as I saw my mother emerge through the doors. Knowing her as I do, I thought, "They won't intimidate her" … and they didn't!

"Search me," I heard my mother say loudly as she continued walking toward me, "I have nothing to hide!" As she stepped aside to be searched, she grinned at the security officer with a cheeky face. "What is this?" I thought as the scene unfolded before me. "What could have made the alarms sound?" As the security officer continued to search my mother, they finally reached into the pockets of her jacket and found her dentures tucked away. Retrieving the dentures from her coat pocket for all to see, we all burst out laughing uncontrollably.

In the end, all was resolved to security's satisfaction and we had a good laugh. The point of this story is about more than being willing to be searched by a stranger because you know you want to travel and have nothing to hide. That day in the midst of noisy alarms ringing and the quiet, stern look of the security personnel as they approached my mother, she had no reservations about being searched. Sometimes we need to have the same attitude towards our inner life – willing to be searched – and see if there is anything that can stop us from travelling safely in this life. David said, "Search me, God, and know my heart; test me and know my anxious thoughts. See if there is any offensive way in me, and lead me in the way everlasting" (Psalm 139:23-24).

A Look at Silence

There are two kinds of silence. On one side, silence can be negative, intimidating and harmful. This is the silence of oppression, a controlling force which leaves victims voiceless and the needy helpless. The second type of silence is addressing your heart and mind to open up and be released to the power of God's presence.

The Power of Stillness

Understanding the power of stillness and applying it to your life can be life changing. It allows you to receive deep healing, and you need the word and the Spirit working together in harmony for that to occur. Stillness detoxifies one's life from all the negative words, events and experiences you have had so you can overcome and learn from them. When we get a revelation of this, it's hard to understand. The harmful silence always keeps you in silence about what's hurting you and what the real issues are. Some people call this denial. Denial doesn't always mean we don't see that there's a problem. Rather, we might rationalise, excuse or minimise its significance or effect upon us.

There are many reasons we use denial, including avoidance of physical or emotional pain, fear, shame or conflict. It's just like a defence. Another reason we deny problems is because they're so familiar to us. Perhaps you grew up with them and don't even recognise that something is wrong. Some express their denial with words like, "I'm not seeing a counsellor," thinking there's nothing to discuss with a professional. I believe that's a great way forward and an approach that merits consideration in some instances. Whether you choose to speak to a professional or bare your heart to God, what I'm referring to is to simply be real with yourself and real with God. You might not be able to do this with everybody, so why not open your heart to God so the healing can take place within you?

How Do I Begin?

We all have anxious thoughts at times. To deal with them, I suggest saying this prayer that David prayed: "Search me, God, and know my heart; test me and know my anxious thoughts" (Psalm 139:23). After you whisper that prayer, take time to be still and write down what comes to your mind.

David the Psalmist is one of my favourite heroes in Scripture. Referred to as a man after God's own heart in 1 Samuel, he was courageous and strong in battle, a man who trusted in God for protection. Yet, he was a man of contrasts – single-minded and devoted to God at times, but also failing miserably and committing serious sins. He messed up big time with Bathsheba when he lusted after her and chose to sleep with someone else's wife. When he discovered that she was pregnant, he feared the truth would come out. He schemed to have her husband brought back from the battlefield to be with Bathsheba, hoping that reuniting them briefly would mask the infidelity that brought about the pregnancy. When King David's plan failed, he plotted to have Uriah, Bathsheba's husband, killed. Facing the consequences of what he had done, David knew it was sinful. Grieved and convicted, he didn't hesitate to accept responsibility. He prayed, "Search my heart, Lord" (Psalm 51), acknowledging his need for forgiveness and healing.

> *My question is this: do you really want to live with that person lurking in the shadows for the rest of your life?*

Perhaps you're not a person who has done much wrong but have had wrong done to you. You can choose to forgive that person and allow God's presence to touch your life and move on rather than remain on that merry-go-round for the rest of life. Everyone has been hurt at times and so often we are tempted to languish in the painful memories of past hurts. When we think about those individuals who have been unkind or hurtful, that pain lingers in the corridors of our minds with relentless fervour. We talk about how we have been wronged at breakfast and before we go to bed, rehearsing over and over what someone has done to us. My question is this: do you really want to live with that person lurking in the shadows for the rest of your life? Failing to release an offence is like having a baby in your arms that goes to bed with you and gets up with you… and you just keep nursing this offence.

David asked God to show him where his faults might lie. If he could be made aware of them before they hurt him or others, why wouldn't he prefer to be changed ahead of time? This is exactly what a person with a tender heart toward God ought to do. He ought to ask God to search his heart so that he can be made aware of anything that needs to be dealt with.

God has given us as the body of Christ a specific time to be introspective, though His desire is that we should deal with sin as quickly as possible all the time.

If you need inner healing, read Jeremiah 17:14-18 in The Message (MSG), which says:

> "God, pick up the pieces. Put me back together again. You are my praise! Listen to how they talk about me: "So where's this 'Word of God'? We'd like to see something happen!" But it wasn't my idea to call for Doomsday. I never wanted trouble You know what I've said. It's all out in the open before you. Don't add to my troubles Give me some relief! Let those who harass me be harassed, not me. Let them be disgraced, not me. Bring down upon them the day of doom. Lower the boom. Boom!"

Today, let your prayer be, "Heal me, oh Lord, that I might be healed." Let that be your heartfelt prayer and put a stop to your pain. Take off the mask of pretence and become the real. You don't have to hide in your pain. As you sit before The Lord, He will heal you. Be still and let His presence fill your heart and mind with freedom and freshness. I've said this prayer from the depths of my heart.

Silence is Strong Medicine

The Bible says, "The Lord is in his holy temple; let all the earth be silent before him" (Habakkuk 2:20). Sadly, silence is perceived as weird in our culture and in the Christian culture. It makes people uncomfortable and many people are intimidated by silence. It may cause you to address issues that you might be running from. However, it is an essential discipline for one's spiritual life in Christ.

Pause for a moment and think about the last time you experienced even just one minute of silent worship in a church service or small group. How long has it been? Being silent is like strong medicine that heals us and transforms us to be more like Christ. Silence makes space for a deeper engagement with God and other people. Many people avoid quiet and stillness because it makes them uncomfortable. If we spend some time before God in silence, the Holy Spirit will bring up into our consciousness whatever sins, burdens or hurts we have repressed. You may find this awareness disturbing, but if we will allow ourselves to be opened by the Spirit in silence, then the healing light of God can reach us and deeply touch us. We can also practise silent prayer with others in community and in this way those who are more mature spiritually can welcome others into being silent together in the presence of God.

Andrew Murray addressed this in his book titled Waiting on God, recognising the need that many Christians feel of being helped to a deeper and clearer insight into all that Christ could be to them. He shows both the need and the benefits of waiting upon God, and of giving God time and place to show us what He can do and what He will do. Murray's underlying theme challenges us to discover how God's loving presence can refresh our weary heart as we learn to wait on Him in stillness and know The Lord of the Silence.

Practising Silence

As a discipline, silence goes with solitude and has two sides: not speaking and not listening to sounds, except perhaps the gentle sounds of nature. When we learn to keep silent, the quiet moves from our environment into our soul and the absence of sound becomes a wonderful realisation of the presence of God as we feel the refreshing wind of eternity blowing gently on our face.

My personal approach to stillness can vary. I learnt everything is a process, including personal quiet moments of reflection and pausing to lean in to hear the gentle whisper that comes from a secret place.

Before I began my search for The Lord of the Silence, I thought the secret place was behind closed doors. However, I have realised over the years it's also a life lived in public with noise and distractions and mega hardships that can challenge us daily.

I have discovered the power of worship and how it brings me to a place of the wow factor of God. It is an atmosphere created in my personal time, that has taught me to enjoy His presence because I feel His presence. The way I feel His presence is through my hands – a heat, a tingling, a numbness, a weight. I used to feel this when I sat as a teenager in prayer in the early hours of the morning around four o'clock. Over the years this experience has stayed with me. Along the journey I desired to not just feel but go beyond that sense of feeling because I've sat still and enjoyed just being in friendship, in fellowship, in communion or whatever word you find comfortable to fit in here. Going beyond a feeling is seeking God for more. The charismatic world has done a lot of damage to the reputation of the work of the Holy Spirit. Some people are afraid to engage in the presence of God and, therefore, miss out on all of God.

I'm not really a touchy-feely person; I wasn't raised that way. But when I had an encounter with God, I soon realised God is pretty much into touchy feely. Especially as we read the book of Acts and through my travels across the nations I have witnessed the touch of God on lives. In Norway after finishing speaking I didn't touch anybody, but the Holy Spirit did. People encountered the presence of God, and I had to ask them to share what was happening to them. Yes, it's real and not spooky. In fact, when you think about it, there are more spooks out there looking and searching for something spiritual, but they're going to the wrong places.

Today I have moments throughout my day in stillness... sometimes ten minutes, sometimes much longer. The key is the desire to want more of Him. That's the first step. The second is simply to spend time with Him without making it a chore. Thirdly, worship helps you forget about you and helps you lean in for longer and frames your time with His presence. This becomes a part of your new normal – and it is a wonderful place to linger, for it is where The Lord of the Silence dwells.

"

When one is at one's wits' end, one sees blood and heartache. In that place of aloneness there is silence… but there is no need to fear, for The Lord of the Silence is with you.

Chapter 10

The Silent Overcomer

Have you ever heard of the domino effect? William Shakespeare penned these words which I believe describes it: "When sorrows come, they come not single spies but in battalions." When one thing goes wrong, it is almost certain that other problems will arise resembling the slide of a stack of dominoes.

Though no one seeks such an experience, some do encounter circumstances that resemble the slide of a stack of dominoes. If 'the domino effect' happens in any area of your life, you will discover very quickly who your real friends are. Sadly, many people do not want to associate with those going through difficulties, and some Christians can be the first to abandon sinking ships like rats on the Titanic. Success often attracts the wrong people and the fickleness of humanity is guaranteed to disappoint you. The silence of despair and constant disappointment screams at you in your darkest hours. Self-doubt and the enemy whispering 'loser' in your ear are constant companions.

Winston Churchill famously said, "If you're going through hell, keep going." The decision to keep going is one thing but based on my experience, you'll need a few more tools in your physical and mental survival kit to endure the onslaught that life can bring your way.

No Flow, No Go

When finances dry up and there is no cash flow, my husband says, "No flow, no go." The essentials of getting around town to meetings, to coffee meetings and lunches and keeping your mobile phone on air can add monumental stress as one navigates the Rivers of Rupture. Small costs are hurdles of inconvenience in the race to the line.

Car Trouble

What happens if, out of the blue, your car blows up on the motorway? What do you do? On one occasion this happened to me. In the end, the Mercedes garage that towed my wreck into their facility replaced it with the latest model. Shortly thereafter, I began to turn up at meetings in that vehicle – the latest model Mercedes – and found that people were so bemused at my apparent success that they began to shower me with more.

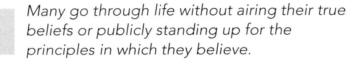

Many go through life without airing their true beliefs or publicly standing up for the principles in which they believe.

Couples, of course, go through these times together and in a family with children, one seeks to protect them from one's pain and paint a fake picture on the canvas of challenge. Children, however, are no fools and their detection instincts and simple minds often are God sent as they comment in their innocence. The truth is that in difficult times there is baggage to carry, whether we like it or not. The load gets heavier and the days get longer. Going to bed exhausted after an extremely busy day is joy, yet insomnia creeps in and you wake up tired.

Renewed and Strengthened

Only much prayer and worship will see you through this. My husband and I would always pray and worship together and we felt His presence come into the room and energise us at our lowest charge levels. He does renew our strength.

Though The Lord of the Silence says that He will never leave us or forsake us, I have seen His face grow further away for a time as I found myself in the midst of a storm. This is a very lonely place to be, yet it can become a place of renewal. It is usually there that He speaks, but you have to be looking for Him and remain attentive as you wait for that whisper. The secret is to 'be still and know'.

There were times that both my husband and I saw the hand of God guiding us at difficult moments and when we feared the rebuke or wrath of our enemy, we noticed that He shut their mouths as He shut the mouths of lions when Daniel stood in the lions' den.

God's Ways

We saw God move at the last second and He was never early; more importantly, He was also never late. In those kinds of situations, we found that the more we tried to solve our problems, the worse it became. The more that we literally let go and left it to Him, the more we saw His miracle intervention power at work. This was particularly true in business-related financial matters. It seems that funds expected always take double the time to arrive and one's faith is stretched to the breaking point.

We learned a great lesson on one occasion when our son Christopher, with his sister, sowed a seed (gave a donation) one day and they went to their room to pray. Shortly thereafter, Christopher told Martin that funds had arrived in his account but Martin insisted that this was not the case.

Christopher remained steadfast, insisting that the funds had arrived because he and his sister had sewn a seed from their savings. Because of his unwavering insistence, we then checked only to find that a large credit had been made. We were in shock that night and found two days later that the money had been credited in error by a bank employee. By that time our awaited funds arrived. We watched in awe as The Lord of the Silence moved in our situation, realising that even the bank employee had a part as God bridged our needs and rewarded the faith of Christopher and his sister.

No Surrender

Another attribute for your survival kit is an attitude of no surrender and never giving up. We must have the kind of faith Abraham had (Romans 4:20) who was "fully persuaded" that God would fulfil His promises to him and do what He said, including giving him a son, even when he and his wife, Sarah, were too old in the natural to bear a child.

A good example of this attitude of no surrender is found in the life of a man named Job. Like a Job experience, my husband and I have experienced attacks on our health as the enemy tried to break us. One occasion that comes to mind found my husband in the middle of a very big business deal, and at short notice, he was expected next day in New York. That morning he awoke and as he stepped out from the bed, he became violently sick and lost his balance due to vertigo. After examining Martin, the visiting doctor said no screens or tests were necessary, just rest for a week. Martin's work was pressing and he had to go to New York so he asked me to pray for him and lay hands on him. I prayed in faith according to God's word, and the next morning he bounced out of bed and was fully healed as he left for Heathrow Airport.

More Than Conquerors

We must carry the word of God with us for, according to Scripture, "… we are more than conquerors through Him who loved us" (Romans 8 v 37). We must declare God's words, and most of all, we must have faith. This faith is a silent faith… a bold, determined faith in The Lord of the Silence, but it is a key survival tool for the overcomer.

To be an overcomer, one must be true to their convictions, which is part of the fabric of who one is at the core. Many go through life without airing their true beliefs or publicly standing up for the principles in which they believe. Their voice and minds hide behind a symbolic parapet, which is a low protective wall built along the edge of a roof or balcony on many of London's structures. Historically, it was intended to help defend the structure against attack. Those who embrace the belief that 'we are more than conquerors through Christ' are willing to come above the parapet and be heard in private and public. To declare one's views is similar to 'nailing one's colours to the mast' or raising your head above the parapet where life's snipers can fire their venomous visitations at you. When faced with the challenge I referred to earlier, we as a family chose to stick our heads above the parapet to defend our family rather than surrender.

Prayer warriors around you are key helpers in defending against attacks, but some grow faint and weary at the times most needed to press in. At the vital moment in Gethsemane the Apostles could not stay awake and pray as Jesus had instructed them to do. As they slept, He was alone as He sweated tears of blood. When one is at wits' end, one sees blood and heartache. In that place of aloneness there is silence… silence in pain… silence in sorrow… but there is no need to fear, for The Lord of the Silence is with you.

Some lessons take time to learn. Our hope lies not in our own ability to hear God, but in His patience with us.

Chapter 11

God in the Night

At one point in my life I was running away from the call of God on my life – a purpose that was very clear at as early an age as 14 years old. I was youth pastor for 10 years and divorce was something I never thought I'd have to walk through, but I did! Sometimes life takes on many twists and turns, and this season of my life left me running away from the church because I found them very judgemental. But deep down, there was a hunger that never left me… the still longing to obey the call. But I decided maybe the best way forward was to be behind closed doors where no one was watching.

Silence and A Cuppa Tea

One evening the leaders of my church asked me to become involved with leading a pastorate group and I was in two minds. Contemplating their request, I was restless and couldn't sleep. As we Brits always do when we're stressed, I decided to have a 'cuppa tea'!

I shared a story in chapter six which I want to revisit for a moment about what I believe to have been a divine encounter. As I sipped my tea, I heard a hushed whisper urging me to turn the TV on. After mentally arguing with myself that God certainly would not be telling me to turn the TV on, I finally conceded after that gentle voice repeated the same thing again. As the television screen came on, I knew instantly God was speaking to me because the words were personal and piercing… and I knew I had to listen!

'Suddenly' is the only suitable word I can think of that can describe the change of atmosphere that happened as God's presence filled the room. (I had never had an experience before nor since that time when turning the television on totally changed the atmosphere!)

It was like a tangible weight of God's glory touched my heart and mind. I knew without a doubt that word was for me, and The Lord of the Silence had prompted my heart to turn on the TV. There in my kitchen, I repented and wept. In a moment, my hands felt a tangible heat on them and my whole body felt like it was on fire. I know for some, this kind of phenomena is hard to understand, and you may think this is strange. But remember, the presence of God is not a theory... it is reality!

I encountered God's presence in a mighty, truly life-changing way that night. That encounter with God was so magnificent and so intimate that words are inadequate to describe what happened within me. It was a turn-around moment in my life because I discovered that God never gives up on you!

Since then I have been traveling, preaching, and teaching the word. That same kind of encounter can be yours too! No matter what life has brought your way, whatever you've walked through or had to overcome, His presence is with you right now as you read this book. Later, my story went live on God TV. I was interviewed in London at an event I was hosting at the time. My friend, God can step into your life in a dynamic, miraculous way too, and He will use any means necessary to reach you. So don't get too religious... I know from personal experience that God speaks and makes His presence real in the strangest places and speaks in the most unusual ways... even in the middle of the night when you are having a cuppa tea!

Don't Limit God

We don't have to put God in a tidy box and tie up the box with a ribbon of preconceived notions about Him. When children play with toys we always ask them to tidy up afterwards. How many times have you said to your children, 'Don't make a mess; put those toys back in the box' because, as a parent, you were trying to teach them good discipline. Yet, when it comes to 'playing/enjoying God', don't be so cautious and 'tidy' that you become afraid to allow yourself to go further and explore the potential in His presence. It is easy to become tidy, but I have learned from personal experience that sometimes, God shows up in your mess. He may not be tidy when His presence shows up. God finds great pleasure in touching you; it's what's He is best at. Stillness of the night that day grabbed my attention and changed the course of my life. So many things grab for our attention every day of our lives, but when God's got you, you're in for a ride of a lifetime!

God is using the media edge in our lives. In regard to all the research, we've got to be where the people are – and that's on Facebook, apps, TV, radio and a host of other emerging media outlets.

Samuel had a similar encounter while sleeping. As he slept, he heard a voice calling his name. Thinking it was Eli, the priest, whom Samuel served in the tabernacle in Shiloh, Samuel went to Eli and said, "Here I am. You called me."

Waking up enough to respond, Eli said, "I didn't call you. Go lie down again." The same thing happened two more times. Samuel went to Eli and once again, Eli sent him back to his sleeping quarters. When he heard his name called a third time, Scripture says, "So he arose and went to Eli, and said, 'Here I am, for you did call me.' Then Eli perceived that the Lord had called the boy. Therefore Eli said to Samuel, 'Go, lie down, and it shall be, if He calls you, that you must say, 'Speak, Lord, for Your servant hears'." (1 Samuel 3:8-9). So Samuel went back to lie down again as Eli had instructed.

Not long after Samuel had returned to his sleeping quarters, Samuel heard a voice saying, "Samuel! Samuel!" And in obedience to Eli's instructions, he responded, "Speak, for Your servant hears." God's instructions to Samuel in the moments that followed changed the course of his life and ushered him into his calling as a prophet.

Today, sleep is one of the weirdest things we do every day. We spend hours unconscious, lying on our beds, while our bodies recharge and our brains process our experiences, sometimes in the form of dreams. But sometimes, our sleep is interrupted just as it was in the example of Samuel. In this account from 1 Samuel 3, we find a young man whose sleep was interrupted. Samuel almost missed the most important moment in his life. The Lord came calling and he thought it was the priest, Eli. Only after coming to Eli for the third time did the priest realise what was happening. God was calling the boy!

> *...I have discovered that God does not give up on us. Instead, He helps us, bears with us and leads us.*

Samuel sought out the wisdom of the elderly man, setting an example for us and demonstrating the importance of mentors. Fortunately, Eli's character was intact enough to offer sage advice. Additionally, the Lord was patient enough to call out to Samuel a fourth time. Without his mentor, Samuel could have lost his greatest opportunity.

Committing to Listen

We can take away two important points from this little episode. 1. God's calling is not always as obvious as we'd like it to be. He does not always grant giant signs, an audible voice or miraculous revelations, visions or encounters. Even in Samuel's case, when God did speak audibly, he had trouble figuring out who was talking to him. The wonderful part of this story is that Samuel did finally identify who was talking to him… and if he did, then we will too!

That means listening to God's voice is not a one-step process, but rather, it involves a serious commitment. We must listen and discern. The message which God is granting to us may be hidden or difficult to understand. Our hearing of Him requires patience, practice, and pressing in… discernment. God could have given up on Samuel after the first time the boy misunderstood the voice. Yet, God spoke again and again until Samuel responded the right way, with readiness. He did not expect Samuel to respond the right way at first, but patiently repeated His call to Samuel until the message sunk in.

Waiting In Silence

We, too, might need God to speak the same thing to us over and over until it sinks in. Some things are difficult to hear. Some lessons take time to learn. Our hope lies not in our own ability to hear God, but in His patience with us. That might be trying to cultivate a prayer of stillness in His presence, inspire of life and failing many times. I have failed so many times, but I have discovered that God does not give up on us. Instead, He helps us, bears with us and leads us. He knows we are limited and imperfect people who need a lot of support and He graciously gives it to us time and again. I relish sleep as a welcome respite, for it gives us relief from the hard work. Why don't you try to do the same?

The next time when you lay your head to rest on the pillow and you sink into your mattress, you might let the silence come over you and allow yourself to listen in the dark for the whisper of The Lord of the Silence. You might just hear the same voice that Samuel did 3,000 years ago.

"

Tune out the noise of the world around you… and begin your journey with The Lord of the Silence. His name is Jesus! When you do, you will never be the same!

Chapter 12

The Journey

As we make our way long life's pathway, we find that pain and trouble are no respecter of persons. These unwelcome guests can visit you at any age and any time in your life. Whether you are rich or poor, in good or bad health, the enemy wants to destroy you and will attack those at any age or any level in society.

A few years ago, my husband and I had this kind of encounter when our experienced protagonist sought to attack us with complete fabricated lies and managed to persuade the authorities to come against us. At our lowest ebb and at the point of being on the ground, the enemy, using this man, came to kick us and lay the final blow of destruction.

We were suddenly faced with the need to defend ourselves and engage an expert in the field of law related to the matter. One lawyer was a member of our church who counselled a quick trial, admission of guilt, plea bargain and payment of his fees. We knew we were innocent so Martin decided to stay in London and fight the case himself in person as a litigant. He dismissed the lawyer, paid him for his services, and went into battle.

The Silent Valentine

Concurrent with Martin's endeavours as a litigant, I went off to preach at several venues in Miami. Back in London, my husband dealt with the situation, taking it as far as he could, after which he came to join me towards the end of my ministry trip.

One Sunday on Valentine's Day, the 14th February, we were both scheduled to speak. As we waited in the hotel lobby to be collected by our hosts, Martin received an email from the High Courts of

England informing him that all charges levied against us had been dismissed and that the Courts had awarded us full recovery of all our costs.

We all know that the High Courts of any nation, let alone England, do not work on a Sunday, but we know that God does. To receive this news 15 minutes before standing upon His platform to speak His message to His people was a truly Valentine Day gift from on High. Eight months of incessant concern and sleepless nights suddenly came to an end on a Sunday with just one email! Relief flowed through our grateful hearts, and as we stood on the platform minutes later, we spoke with the authority of heaven, knowing that The Lord of the Silence had intervened in our situation.

Never Give Up!

I share this story to encourage you to follow your convictions, to never give up hope when it seems that all are against you, and to always remember that we serve a God who created the Earth, the days and the life we have. His watchful eye is forever upon us; He never slumbers nor sleeps. That day is forever etched in our memories as we were reminded that The Lord of the Silence works on Sundays – sometimes in the most unexpected ways and at the most extraordinary times! He is there for us all at the point of our need, and He does not leave us or forsake us.

...I saw the biggest turnaround and the greatest breakthrough in my life. This breakthrough came as no accident, but from a seed sewn in my life some 18 years ago...

Since then, our Valentine Day date has been renamed Victory Valentine Day. Later, I did enquire as to how the email was sent to me on a Sunday, but even the Court clerks could not offer plausible explanation and the costs clerk was totally bemused and I can still hear him saying, "I just don't understand..."

The Silent Thief

As a successful, dynamic businessman, my husband has helped many in his business and acted in numerous global transactions. He is a man of integrity who treats people with respect and dignity, which in most instances is reciprocated. In one instance, however, one of his clients did not act honourably, but stole an over seven-figure sum from us through fraudulent means. With the thought of trying to achieve a quick resolution, we stupidly agreed to use the same lawyer, but unfortunately, that only facilitated the theft further.

The loss of the money was one thing, but the fact that the client who had acted so dishonourably was a Jewish man with whom my husband had shared intimate details of our faith walk, the Bible and Torah made the experience gutting. Our Rabbi friend from Jerusalem wrote to the Chief Rabbi in the UK, but his attempt to broker a peaceful solution also failed.

A Different Kind of Silence

For my husband and me, it seemed that once again the religious leaders did not want to engage in real life issues but pontificate from and on the walls where they sat. We were both raised to bless the Jew but in doing so in this instance, we were cheated. My husband had realised many millions in a real estate transaction for the man, but the greed of humanity steamrolled the ethics and morals of the man.

Martin and I prayed for relief and restoration, but to date, it has not come. However, we are at peace knowing that God will vindicate us at some point. The man in question was found to be a serial offender and as I write this book, others are also being tortured by his hand and actions.

Many of our friends are Jewish and the behaviour of the man who came against us was not the norm. However, a Jew will never judge a fellow Jew, and the silence of the Rabbi was deafening and disappointing for us, just as it was for Jesus, who watched his fellow Jewish leaders remain silent to the injustice He suffered at the hands of His accusers before Pilate. As He was led to Golgotha and his hands and feet were nailed to the cross with rough-hewn nails, the Jewish leaders kept their silence as He hung suspended between Earth and heaven between two thieves.

As ethics and principles fail under leadership that fails to act, we begin to see why our societies slowly disintegrate and why the fibre of faith is torn and ruined. This should not become a point of discouragement, but should guide our steps to remain true to the path of truth and righteousness.

The Unfolding Journey

The writing of this book started in early 2019, probably at a time the rogue virus COVID-19 was hatching, plotting to bring about the biggest global shutdown ever known. The book finishes as we begin to witness a second wave of activity and rumours of a vaccine. Pandemic has become almost a way of life and a dress rehearsal of more to come.

The Lord of the Silence used the pause button to remind us all of life's fragility and that those that take the things of life for granted may well be taken. Statistics change each day as the death toll continues to rise. We are told that The Lord of the Silence never slumbers nor sleeps in Psalm 121:4 and nothing that happens is without reason (Ecclesiastes 3).

As I reflect on lockdown from a personal perspective, I see that COVID-19 now into 2020 and beyond, was a period in my life that I will never forget for it was the time that I saw the biggest turnaround and the greatest breakthrough in my life. This breakthrough came as no accident, but from a seed sewn in my life some 18 years ago when despite great odds, I stepped out to do something out of the box and out of the ordinary.

These last 18 years were at times a nightmare, yet we as a family ploughed our furrow, kept our head down, and waited with the faith of a mustard seed for The Lord of the Silence to come through. This He did in a spectacular way, in an unimaginable circumstance… above and beyond what anyone could have created or dreamed possible. It was a moment when the Earth opened into the realm of exceedingly and abundantly – so brilliant my heart cannot contain it all.

The Journey Continues

In short, The Lord of the Silence spoke and all heaven broke loose in my life. This and what happened next is so magnificent that it will require more pages than this book can hold. Hence, it will be the subject of my next book – a story of complete helplessness, hopelessness and hurt hewn from an impenetrable rock and sculpted by The Lord of the Silence into a beautiful story of restoration.

Each step of this journey has brought me closer to The Lord of the Silence, and learning to 'be still and know' has drawn me to a place unlike anything I had ever experienced – a place of solemn stillness and wonder as the glorious symphony of heaven, though silent, resounds like crashes of thunder in my heart! I now run to this sanctuary of silence where I have discovered the eternal treasure of relationship with The Lord of the Silence, so deep and indescribably personal that it has become the foundation of my life.

This Is Your Time

The Lord of the Silence is waiting for you to take the first step. Will you put down your pen of pain used for entries in your registry of wounds and surrender the painful memories of yesterday to The Lord of the Silence? When you do, His peace will blow upon your life like a cool, refreshing breeze. His presence will cover you like a warm blanket and wrap you in His love and splendour. You will find rest and peace like you have never known before.

This treasure awaits you. It is as close as your next breath. Make a decision today to tune out the noise of the world around you – the crisis-laden news reports, the pinging of mobile devices, the weariness of lockdown – and begin your journey with The Lord of the Silence. His name is Jesus! When you do, you will never be the same!

About the Author

Born in London, of Indian descent, and from a Hindu Punjabi background, Shaneen enjoyed a Christian-based education and attended Sunday school as a little girl, even though her parents did not formally embrace the teachings of the Christian faith until Shaneen was older. Her early years found her caught between the traditions of her heritage and the gentle voice of The Lord of the Silence that called to her.

Her journey in life has taken her from tradition to self-discovery and divine purpose, resulting in a timeless message that is relevant today for the faith-based community and corporate multi-culture audiences of all ages. Shaneen has spent years helping others discover their purpose, identify their passion in life, and release their gifts to fulfil their dreams. For nearly three decades, she has travelled the world as a speaker and frequent host on Christian television and radio, both in the UK and America. She and her husband, Martin, live in London, England.

Scan Me!

For information about other books and products by Shaneen Clarke, guest appearances, or booking details for speaking engagements and conferences/live and virtual, visit ShaneenClarke.com.

For a complete list of media resources by Shaneen Clarke, visit ShaneenClarke.com.

Dare To Be Great and The Lord of the Silence are also available on Amazon.

Printed in Great Britain
by Amazon